Arnold Grummer's Complete

Paper Casting

Arnold and Mabel Grummer

Published by

kp krause publications
An Imprint of F+W Publications

700 East State Street • Iola, WI 54990-0001
715-445-2214 • 888-457-2873
www.krausebooks.com

Please call or write for our free catalog of publications. Our toll-free number to place an order or obtain a free catalog is 800-258-0929 or please use our regular business telephone 715-445-2214 for editorial comment and further information.

Library of Congress Catalog Number 2001099521
ISBN 13-digit: 978-0-87349-425-0
ISBN 10-digit: 0-87349-425-3

Dedication

This book is dedicated to Kim, our daughter, who conceived the book, and whose energy and counsel led it from nothing to something wonderful.

Acknowledgments

Aspects of this book, and the general environment that accompanied its development, owe a debt of gratitude to the artistic and technical, and seemingly endless, creative resources of Spencer Rotzel. May his graphic world be always available in our moments of crisis.

Introduction to Paper Casting: The World of Non-sheet Forms

Among other things, non-sheet forms of paper are not a new thought.

When I was Curator of the Dard Hunter Paper Museum (now the Robert C. Williams American Museum of Papermaking), we had a stunningly beautifully decorated paper coffin in one of our huge display cases of Eastern artifacts. It was only large enough to accommodate a small mummified falcon, which lay partially within it. Such accommodation of the bird was, as I remember, the whim of a Persian Nobleman with equal amounts of affection for the bird and discretionary cash. At my time of association with it as curator, the coffin was centuries old.

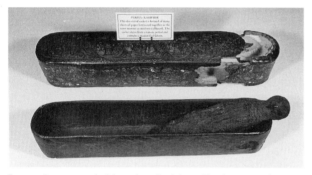

Two-part paper casket for a favorite falcon. The foreground section containing the mummified falcon fits into the background section. The attached museum card reads, "This decorated casket is formed of many sheets of paper laminated together in the same manner as modern wallboard. The casket dates from a remote period and contains a mummified falcon." From the collection of the Robert C. Williams American Museum of Papermaking.

Institute of Paper Chemistry paper house.

A more recent and much larger non-sheet paper form was the "paper house," developed and built at the former Institute of Paper Chemistry in Appleton, Wisconsin, as part of WWII research. It was designed to house four people, could be packaged in 2 by 4 by 8 feet for mass air shipment, and could be erected by one man without tools. Its purpose was to help provide shelter for European WWII refugees. It was

The first paper: a wasp's nest.

erected on the Institute campus in 1944 and disassembled in 1952 to make way for a new building. For eight years, it withstood Wisconsin winter blizzards and summer storms.

Obviously, then, non-sheet forms of paper are actually "old hat." In fact, paper's past is dotted with exciting and amazing non-sheet forms, which include paper wheels for train cars, a paper church in Sweden, racing punts for Ivy League colleges, paper coffins for people, and many more. Some are cataloged in Dard Hunter's master book of paper history, *Papermaking: The History and Technique of an Ancient Craft*. Further, the first recognized "paper" was a wasp's nest, not a flat sheet.

So indeed, don't be stalled in the flat sheet syndrome. Let your imagination roam and soar into all kinds of shapes, forms, and contours as small as a delicate earring or as big as a church in Sweden.

Arnold E. Grummer

Table of Contents

Chapter One

What is Paper Casting?

Cast paper embellished with ultra-fine glitter by Barbara Trombley.

Chapter

1

Non-sheet paper forms can be structured in several ways. One of the easiest, most versatile, delicate, and delightful is paper casting, particularly with cotton linters. By definition, paper casting is piling up, or by other means arranging, soaking wet fibers into a desired shape or form and keeping them there until dry.

Working or getting the soaking wet fibers into a form or shape might not be all that difficult, but it can be tricky to keep them in that shape or form while they dry and become strongly enough bonded to stay that way. The whole process is simplified by having a form or shape of rigid, waterproof material to put the mass of wet fibers (pulp) in, on, or around. The form then supports and keeps the wet mass in the proper shape as, and until, it dries. Ultimately then, by paper casting you can duplicate in "paper" (cellulose fibers, that is) any shape or form on the face of the earth, or any you can yourself create in a proper material.

All kinds of ready-made craft-to-high-art shapes are readily at hand in the form of cookie cutters, boxes, dimensional art, carvings, dimensional surfaces, botanicals such as the gingko leaf, and so forth. A huge number of utilitarian shapes and forms can be found in a variety of packaging and packaging components, as well as a whole array of fast food containers and compartmental trays, from fluted sundae containers and take-home sandwich boxes to plastic packaging from grocery store delis and bakeries. Then there are bowls from your kitchen or china shelves.

Paper-cast desk art.

Many of these are quite ornamental, as well as useful, when rendered as a paper casting. The possibilities are endless! But industry has beaten you to many of them: egg cartons, food trays, carriers for multiple drinks, and so on.

Fast food tray; an industry paper casting.

The shape or form to which pulp is to be applied is generally referred to as a "mold" (either commercial or home-made, as described on page 13); however, the word "mold" generally does not bring to mind a whole host of items of which, or from which, paper castings can be made. To identify these things not normally associated with "mold," this book sought some other name.

The word "armature" has been applied to large, complex forms upon which paper castings have been based, but the word seems a bit overblown

Bowl matrix and resulting paper cast bowl.

and grandiose for smaller, simpler, and more common items. Personally, we like "matrix." Its definition in *Merriam Webster's Collegiate Dictionary*, Tenth Edition, includes "Something ... from which something else originates, develops, or takes form." Consequently, in this book, such non-flat mold items as dishes, fast food containers, etc., will be identified as a matrix.

For a special look and character, cotton linters are readily available from stores or the vendors listed on page 95. But you will never run out of free pulp, because all of the world's waste paper is pulp (simply laid out and dried in sheet form, the same as new pulp sheets). It's yours to use for a blender, water, and 30 seconds of your time.

For the ultimate in whiteness and delicacy, you will at some time or other want to buy and try cotton linters (you will still need the blender, water, and 30 seconds of your time). But in the matter of waste paper, industry is beating you again. It is scooping up the world's waste paper by the ton to disperse back into pulp for new paper products that include the world's finest printing papers.

In your casting, as in flat sheet papermaking, your merest effort will result in a very adequate final product. More time, effort, care, and added creative talent will move the final product correspondingly higher, even to the uppermost realms of "art."

Go for it!

Common matrices for paper castings.

Chapter Two

Make a Paper Cast in Minutes!

Cast paper made with crushed mica sparkles.

Chapter

2

We know there are those of you out there who would rather get started now on making a paper cast than wait until after reading the entire book. This chapter is for you! To find out more about choosing linter squares and molds, consult Chapter 3.

❋ Supplies

Many of the supplies you need for paper casting should be readily available—you probably already have some in your kitchen! Thoroughly wash all equipment after use, or, if desired, dedicate necessary equipment to paper casting.

You Will Need

Casting mold or matrix
Cotton linter casting squares, other
    linters, or selected waste paper
Kitchen blender
Tea strainer, wire mesh
Sponge
Toweling, terrycloth, and/or paper towels
Measuring cup
Water

❋ The Basic Steps

The basic process is quite simple!

1 Tear off enough cotton linter casting squares, other cotton linters, or six thicknesses of waste paper to cover the selected mold.

2 Put the linters or waste paper in the blender with 3 cups of water.

3 Blend on low for several seconds, then on high for 45 seconds.

4 Pour the blender's contents (pulp) into the tea strainer; let drain into the measuring cup. **Note:** Save the water for your next casting.

5 Plop pulp directly from the strainer onto the mold.

2   4   5

6 Jiggle the pulp gently with your hand, shaking the fibers into the mold's details. Maintain uniform thickness as much as possible.

7 Press firmly with your hand to settle the pulp and squeeze out the water.

8 Remove water with a sponge, pressing pulp into every detail of the mold.

9 Use a terrycloth or paper towel to remove as much water and moisture as possible.

✳ Drying

For final drying, there are three options. First, you can carefully peel the cast from the mold and let it air dry. Second, you can leave the cast on the mold and place it in a 275-degree oven (if the mold selected can stand heat). Usually the casting will start to lift from the mold when dry. Check it after 10 minutes; drying time depends on cast thickness. Finally, you can check the mold manufacturer's guidelines regarding microwave use; if the mold will withstand microwave use, follow the guidelines at right.

With your first paper casting tucked safely into your scrapbook, let's expand the paper casting scene.

Using a Microwave to Dry a Paper Cast

1. Put microwave on medium setting.
2. Microwave for 1 minute.
3. Give mold one-quarter turn.
4. Microwave for 30 seconds. Repeat 30-second intervals until dry. **Note:** Many casts will dry in 2 minutes.

Caution! The mold will be hot from microwaving—take care when handling. Also, prolonged microwaving can cause scorching.

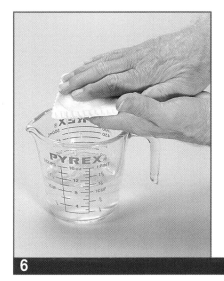

6

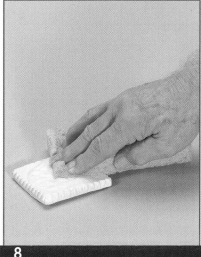

8

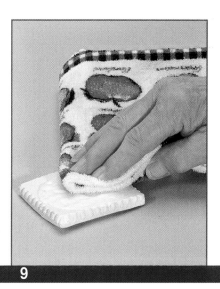

9

Chapter Three

Paper Casting Basics

Cast paper highlighted with raised ink pads.

Chapter

3

❋ Choosing a Mold

This is one of the most important decisions you will have to make when casting paper. Commercial molds are available in three types: plastic, flexible, and rigid.

Plastic

Plastic molds can produce a two-dimensional cast. Plastic cookie cutters or candy molds often have interesting detail that will emboss the surface of the finished cast. Hundreds of designs are available in plastic, varying in size from a few inches to a few feet. Plastic, with its hard, shiny surface, is easy to work with because release of the paper casting from the mold causes few problems. While many images are available, plastic is usually lacking in detail, which may be a disadvantage.

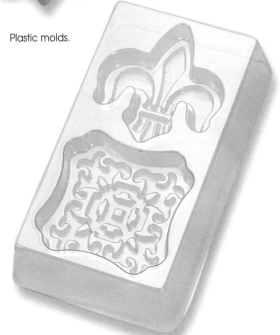

Plastic molds.

Flexible

Flexible molds of latex, silicones, urethanes, and other compounds are also available. Flexible molds allow three-dimensional pieces of art, some with undercuts, because of their good strength and elasticity. Because cotton linters and recycled papers start out as such a watery medium, requiring much pressure for water removal, flexible molds are difficult to use. Also, these molds require backup support, such as sand, to keep from distorting the shape.

Rigid

Rigid molds of terra cotta, or other fired clays or ceramics, come in many sizes and depths. These molds are marketed with multi-purpose uses, such as paper casting, cookie stamping, metal embossing, or casting of various products to make jewelry. Rigid molds are the most desirable molds for paper casting. The casting process and papermaking system require lots of water and lots of pressing and patting; the rigid mold provides a compatible surface, along with fine detail and depth. With care, the molds can be used over and over and will produce a clear, interesting finished product, ready for various art applications and useful gift projects.

Rigid molds.

✳ Pulp Choices

Now that you've chosen what type of mold you want to use, you need to decide on pulp. Paper casters have two choices: 1) pulp by recycling paper, or 2) cotton linters or other new pulp.

A general guideline ratio of waste paper to water in a blender for recycling is one torn-up 8-1/2- by 11-inch sheet of paper to a blender nearly filled with water. Run the blender until chunks of paper are no longer visible.

Pulp by Recycling

Any pulp (fibers) will make castings. The wealth of originally expensive, and expensively refined, pulp in your wastebasket as waste paper will give high-art castings, and a variety of castings in terms of characteristics. Professionally dyed colored pulp is abundant and free in the form of thrown-away colored paper.

As stated in all of Arnold's books, all paper is merely wet pulp that has been laid out on a screen and dried, so every last square inch of waste paper (paper that has been used once) is *dried pulp*. Simply putting this "dry pulp" in a blender with water, and dispersing the fibers (just as must be done with *new* dry pulp), turns it right back into the wet pulp the papermaker put into the head box of the paper machine at a paper mill. Waste *paper* is not waste *fibers*.

Waste paper and wet pulp.

Cotton Linters

Cotton linters have become the "fiber of choice" for paper casting, but a cast can be created by any fiber/pulp. Experience and observation, rather than any scientific study that we're aware of, has made linters a favorite. Fibers from different plants do indeed have different physical characteristics. Even cotton rag fibers (first cutting from the cotton boll) and cotton linter fibers (second or later cutting) are definitely different. But matching the best fiber characteristics to a specific end use is a very scientific undertaking indeed, and scientific research these days is immensely expensive.

Cotton linters' ascendancy as the choice for casting has been aided by repeated expression of personal preference by practicing crafts people and artists. The preference is easily explained. Linters' exceptional whiteness (processor induced) and their exceptional delicacy in the final casting provide characteristics most desired in castings. The whiteness amplifies shadows, which are what tell the eye there is dimensionality. The fragile delicacy of the cotton linter casting is a thing to wonder at and behold. Cotton linters sold for casting have been appropriately "beaten," modifying the fiber. Short fibers are most desirable for casting because they can enter the casting's most minute detail. Overall, many casting molds include very minute details, which mean exceedingly small crevices and niches. Therefore, the shorter and more "limp" (capable of flexing) a fiber is, the more it is capable of being inserted into tiny crevices and niches.

Tips for Casting With Cotton Linters

Linters are a wonderful fiber for paper casting, because the fibers easily form a strong natural bond. When the water is drained away from the mass of wet fibers, the mass is already forming a workable pulp that can be easily handled. The shrinkage rate of the drying pulp is very low, which helps preserve the detail of the mold.

In summation, any fiber, new or out of your wastebasket, can be used for paper casting. Cotton linters sold for casting (it can be assumed) have been appropriately refined (beaten). Very likely you will choose both purchased cotton linters and the wealth of wastebasket fibers. Certainly for Paper Casting With Everyday Objects, Chapter 5, the resources in your wastebasket will give you a broad range of colors and hues—and are free!

✳ Types of Linters

Cotton linters are available in four forms: dry sheet pulp, perforated squares, pre-shredded bulk, and liquid pulp.

Dry Sheet Pulp

This generally comes in precut sheets from as small as 7 by 9 inches to as large as 32 by 38 inches. For use, it is reduced to 2-inch pieces, soaked for several minutes, then run in a blender with plenty of water. Never more than a 5- by 8-inch section should be placed in the blender at one time.

Dry pulp sheet.

Perforated Squares

Cotton linter casting squares are dry sheet pulp in sheets of 1-inch squares. Two-ounce sheets measure 12 by 12 inches, or 144 1-inch squares, of cotton linter pulp. Perforated squares make it easy to pre-measure pulp. To have the right amount, lay the sheet of squares over the mold and tear along the outline of the mold's image. To make a 5-1/2- by 8-1/2-inch sheet or cast, use 45 squares of pulp with 4 cups of water in the blender. Do not exceed 45 squares in the blender at any one time. **Note:** This book uses linter squares in most examples because they are the easiest to use.

Perforated cotton linter casting squares.

Pre-shredded Bulk

This pulp is dry sheet pulp that has been pre-shredded, making it easier to use. Pre-shredding adds to the cost, but has the advantage of being very blender friendly; no soaking is required. For paper casting, use 1/4 cup of loosely packed linter for a 3- by 3-inch cast; adjust measurement for larger casts. Do not exceed 1 cup of linter in the blender at a time.

Pre-shredded cotton linters.

Liquid Pulp

Pre-beaten and pre-blended cotton linter pulp is available by the bucket and can be ordered and shipped from the vendors listed on page 95. Pulp can be ordered with sizing or other additives included. Follow the directions from the supplier for use and storage tips.

Regardless of what pulp is used (cotton linter or recycled paper), the good news is that should a paper casting fail, the linters can be re-dispersed in a blender for another attempt or project.

Tinting Linters

While a bright white linter cast is often preferable, many individuals like to tint pulp. Here are some things to try:

- Tint cotton linters with colored tissue paper and napkins. Add small pieces of tissue, napkins, or colorful paper to linters in the blender until the desired hue is reached.
- Add a pinch of dyed cotton specialty pulps or exotic fibers marketed by several papermaking suppliers (see page 95).
- Experiment with fabric dyes, such as Rit.
- The authors do not recommend construction paper (its dye can stain the mold or matrix), food coloring (ineffective and stains), and acrylic paints (ineffective and foams in the blender).

You can tint white cotton linters with a wide variety of colored papers.

✳ Additives

Assorted additives (from left to right): calcium carbonate, kaolin clay, and methylcellulose.

Anything added to fibers in a pulp is called an additive. Each additive has a specific purpose and creates at least a minutely different paper. A listing of all additives and their purposes used in papermaking would take volumes! For craft and art purposes, most inquiries concern hardening a casting's surface in order that graphics (painting, tinting, and drawing) can be applied. For use of any additive, follow the directions that come with the product.

Wax Sizing Via Addition of Waxed Paper Fibers

Many bleached-white bakery sacks are made of heavily waxed paper. Adding some of this paper to cotton linters or other pulp for casting delivers wax sizing to the casting. It has a definite effect on a casting's surface hardness. The more waxed paper added, the harder the surface. The sizing factor prevents feathering and wicking of liquid paints and inks. Using waxed paper from a roll is not as satisfactory.

Methylcellulose

This sizing agent has mixed reviews for use in castings. Besides providing sizing, it is also an adhesive and can cause release problems for a casting. Factors including the mold surface and the amount of methylcellulose added will affect results. Follow supplier recommendations for preparation and use. Pay meticulous attention to a release agent.

Commercial Sizes

Commercial sizes other than methylcellulose are available from some of the vendors listed on page 95. **Note:** There is internal and external sizing. Internal is the addition of sizing to pulp *before* product formation, while external is the addition *after* product formation.

Calcium Carbonate

Calcium carbonate is a hard (ground limestone) filler. Some of what is added will be deposited at the surface of a casting. This lends some surface hardness and alters normal fiber relationships. Calcium carbonate also is a plus for permanency concerns.

Bakery sacks are made of heavily waxed paper.

Papermakers Clay

The State of Georgia is slowly disappearing into paper; that is because it is a prime source of kaolin clay. For this book's purposes, what is said about calcium carbonate and a casting's surface can be said about papermakers clay; however, clay does not have the effect on permanency that calcium carbonate has and it may give paper casts a grayish tinge.

External Polyurethane Spraying

Empirical observation of spraying clear polyurethane lightly on the face of a cotton linter paper casting showed a very "closed," hard-sized, and firm surface. We suggest experimenting on small, easy-to-make castings to test results with a particular art medium.

❋ Release Agents

Sometimes when one tries to pull or lift a dry casting from its mold, part or much of the casting sticks to the mold's surface; the casting does not "release." Consequently, people look for a release agent, something to cause a dry casting to release easily and completely, that is applied to the mold's surface prior to applying the fibers (pulp). Most often, the agent is a liquid applied by wiping or spraying, but some are in wax or gel form.

The interface between wet pulp and a mold's surface is a very sensitive, scientifically complicated physical area. Its study is not easy, and no easy one-sentence generality will ever define it. The interface contact action is so sensitive that every fiber from a different source, every slight variation in the refinement of a fiber, and every different combination of fibers and additives can affect interface parameters.

Consequently, what might work in one instance possibly might not work in the next. The amount and temperature of water present when the pulp is applied, the amount of pressure applied to the pulp, fast or slow drying, fiber shrinkage characteristics (long fibers cause more overall shrinkage than short ones), and other nuances will affect whether or not a particular casting will release easily or with difficulty.

So the thing to do is listen to others and try what is reported as being successful; note in one's own experience what pulps on what surfaces release easily; try products sold by reputable, knowledgeable vendors; and do your own experimenting.

The same cotton linters that release satisfactorily *without* additives might present more of a release problem *with* additives or tinting materials. If a paper casting shows signs of not releasing, a very thin, sharp blade might help. Slip the thin blade under the casting at some place along its edge and proceed with a delicate touch and great caution to combine lifting and use of the blade. Severe sticking is unfortunately a harbinger of a paper casting fatality.

If castings stick to a mold in whole or in part, the casting mold might need to be cleaned. Scrub with a stiff brush, or if it is a ceramic mold, boil it in water for 10 minutes.

A variety of release agents.

Make sure you apply a release agent before applying pulp.

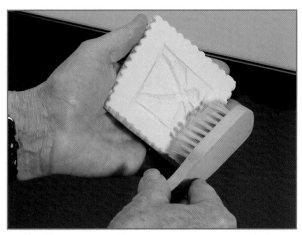

Before its next use, clean a mold with a stiff brush if castings stick to it.

Common Release Agents

Release agents are not extensively discussed or mentioned in available literature, but the following are commonly reported as having been used:
- Glycerin
- Non-stick vegetable spray
- Paste wax
- Silicon spray
- Vaseline diluted with mineral spirits

Silicon spray is easily available, is mostly inorganic, and is least invasive of both the paper and mold. It is easily applied and minimally messy.

Observe safety practices as described on the labels of all of the above. The amount of any release agent applied should be minimal; no puddle of any spray should be left. A light wipe with an absorbent material will eliminate excess.

❋ Drying Paper Casts

The general drying options are presented on page 11, but here is a more in-depth discussion.

Large Castings

Large castings can be placed in a dry, warm place where there is little air movement; a small area with a dehumidifier is excellent. Air movement can cause uneven drying, which means uneven shrinking, which can mean "warping." Fans can be used if a terrycloth towel or similar fabric is placed over the casting.

A large casting might be dry on the outside, but not on the inside. Removal before the entire casting is dry can result in cracking or release problems. Drying time might run from hours to days, depending on size and thickness.

Large castings will need to be weighted on the edges so that the paper casting dries flat. Weights should be something that cannot be damaged by water.

Small Castings

Small castings and bowls can be placed in sunshine inside or out, on or adjacent to heat sources, in ovens that have a light bulb, and so forth. Too much heat for too long a time can cause discoloring, especially at thin edges. Small castings can sometimes be peeled off before entirely dry and then dried free from the mold; however, if any release problem arises, continue drying on the mold.

Microwave Ovens

Be careful about microwave ovens! Check and follow the manufacturer's microwave recommendations carefully for any mold. See page 11 for more specific information.

❋ Surface Decoration

While many perceive the beauty of a paper casting to be found in the image that appears in a pure white, dimensional surface, others might enjoy experimenting with decorative surface treatments using a variety of art materials. The examples on these pages provide just a sampling of finishes possible on a dry paper casting's surface.

The following factors can affect clarity of the casting's image detail, absorption or feathering of surface applications, and brilliance or color retention when decorating cast paper: additives in cotton linter pulp; the use of recycled fiber; and the application of fixatives, coatings, or varnishes to the cast before decoration.

Surface Application Ideas

Here is a list of suggested surface application to help you get started:

- Chalk. Apply with foam or sponge applicators or synthetic cotton balls. Multi-color eye shadow pallets will also work.
- Ink pads. Small raised inkpads or duo color pad markers are easy to use because they can be applied to just the raised details of a cast.
- Spray paint. Metallic, monochromatic color can be dramatic. Be sure to read warnings on labels and use in a well-ventilated area.
- Acrylic paint. Will not feather, even on an untreated paper cast.
- Markers. These come in both watercolor and permanent inks in a host of tip configurations. As a general rule, markers will feather unless an additive is used or the casting's surface is sprayed with a fixative or sealant.

Scrapbook page designed by Debra S. Beagle. Cotton linter pulp is an acid-free fiber. An acid-free buffer for paper-making is also available.

- Glitter. Exceptionally fine glue applicator tips and a panorama of ultra-fine glitter deliver new possibilities for ornate detail and coloration. See page 64 for more information.
- Spray glitter. When just a hint of pearlescence or festive sparkle is needed, try spray glitter. It may be beneficial to use a surface sealant before applying. Again, check all labels and use in a well ventilated area.
- Gilding (most commonly known as gold leaf). Follow directions on adhesive size designed specifically for gilding applications.
- Pearl-Ex (lustrous metallic or pearlescent finish). This comes in a powder form and must be mixed with another art medium before application. Mix with acrylic matte or gloss medium to paint on; mix with acrylic matte or gloss medium and a little bit of water to use a mouth atomizer for a spray finish; and apply with a Dove Blender by dipping the applicator directly into the container and then applying to the desired area.

Gift boxes by Christine Meissner.

Seasons by Susan Pickering Rothamel. Cast paper finished with gilding.

When adhering a dried paper cast to another surface, any household or craft glue should be suitable (check the manufacturer's suggested uses if in doubt).

Post-It® Notebooks

These fun little notebooks make great gifts!

You Will Need

Lightweight cardboard or shirtboard
Medium-weight paper, any color
Post-It® notepad
Double-stick tape
Paper cast, embellished in any desired manner
18 inches of satin ribbon, any color
Pencil
Ruler
Craft glue
Scissors

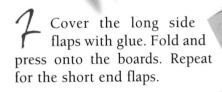

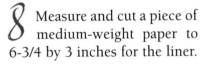

1 Cut the cardboard or shirtboard to the following: two squares 3-1/4 by 3-1/4 inches and one strip 3/8 by 3-1/4 inches.

2 Draw a 7-inch horizontal line at least 1 inch from the bottom of the medium-weight paper (Figure 1).

3 Glue the cardboard covers and spine along the 7-inch line (Figure 2).

4 Cut around the pieces, 5/8 inch from the edge on all sides (Figure 3).

5 Cut square notches at each corner (Figure 4).

6 Make a dot 5/8 inch from the notches on both ends (Figure 4). Cut diagonally from the dots to the corners to create end flaps (Figure 5).

7 Cover the long side flaps with glue. Fold and press onto the boards. Repeat for the short end flaps.

8 Measure and cut a piece of medium-weight paper to 6-3/4 by 3 inches for the liner.

9 Cover the liner with glue. Center and attach over the boards and flaps (Figure 6). Let dry completely.

10 Gently score and fold at the spine joints.

These elegant greeting cards are a snap to make! Simply glue an embellished paper cast to a folded piece of cardstock.

11 Secure the notepad with double-stick tape to the back inside cover.

12 Glue the finished paper cast to the front cover.

13 Wrap the ribbon around the spine and tie in a bow.

medium-weight paper

7 inches long

Figure 1

Figure 2

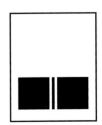

Figure 3

Figure 4

Figure 5

Figure 6

Chapter Four

Pulp Application Methods

Chapter

4

Putting pulp on a small mold is quite easy, and a simple way is described in Chapter 2. On bigger molds, bowls, carvings, or other objects, applying pulp can be a bit more of an undertaking. Below is a range of ways to apply pulp. **Note:** It is best to apply a release agent before applying pulp.

The directions below refer to removing sufficient water so that a pulp patty or sheet can be handled. This is somewhat of a two-edged sword: if too much water is removed, the bond between individual patties and sheets gets very weak, but if not enough water is removed, the patty or sheet can't be handled. Remove no more water than is necessary. Re-wet the patty and sheet edges after application. Press with a sponge. By doing this, you will have re-strengthened the bond between individual patties.

Pulp Plop

Were water not drained from pulp, it obviously would not stay on any surface. Enough water should be drained so it is a soggy mass that can be flattened into shapes. For smaller pulp amounts, an efficient method is to pour the wet pulp into a strainer and shake it back and forth, making the water drain rapidly and forming the pulp into something of an oval ball. This can be plopped onto a surface, or it can be plopped out of the strainer onto the palm of the other hand, squeezed flat between two hands, and then applied to a surface.

Plopping pulp onto a mold directly from a strainer.

Pulp Pieces

An easy way to get pulp onto a mold is to first pour pulp from a blender into a strainer, letting water drain into a pail or bowl. Next, pull pieces or chunks of pulp from the strainer. Finally, layer the pieces evenly across the surface.

Laying pulp pieces onto a mold.

Pulp Patties

When working with pulp patties, pour the pulp from the blender into the strainer, letting water drain into a pail or bowl. Now, dump the pulp on any flat surface. With your hands, flatten the pulp into a patty of reasonable uniform thickness; patting it with a firm bristled brush is helpful. (**Note:** Remove water with your hands and then with a sponge, and if necessary terrycloth towel and paper toweling, until the pulp patty can be handled. Do not discard wet toweling! Dry and re-use it.) Finally, place the patty on the mold or matrix surface.

Flattening a pulp patty.

You can make larger patties by dumping several strainers of pulp on top of, or next to and overlapping, each other. Also, your hands can work patties into various shapes, including round, square, oblong, heart, or irregular. Make shapes to fit open spaces in the mold.

✳ Pulp Sheets Made With a Deckle

What is a deckle? Part of a hand papermaking mold, a deckle is a way to corral fibers over a screen. If you want a round, rectangular, or square sheet, you build a round, rectangular, or square corral. The corral "fence" is a rim of some material that rests on a screen. It can rise above the screen to whatever height is desired. A deckle on top of a screen that is resting on a screen support makes a papermaking hand mold. If the deckle rises high enough, liquid pulp can be poured into it (directly onto a screen). The water drains through the screen, leaving the pulp as a layer/sheet on the screen. It will, of course, be the same shape as the deckle. Deckles are an efficient way of making pulp sheets to put on molds and matrices.

If a papermaking *pour* hand mold is available (see "pour" and "dip" hand papermaking molds in *Arnold Grummer's Complete Guide to Easy Papermaking*), it can be placed in a tub containing 2 or 3 inches of water, and the pulp poured into it. The pulp is evenly distributed in the hand mold, which is then lifted from the water. This forms a sheet on the hand mold's screen. The screen and sheet can be removed from the hand mold and placed on a drain rack in a tray. A piece of window screen is placed over the sheet for protection, and water can be removed by pressing with a sponge. Sandwiched between the two screens, the sheet can be flipped over and the papermaking screen (now on top) can be removed. The sheet can be applied as a whole, or pieces can be pulled and applied as described on page 23.

Pouring cotton linter into the deckle of a hand mold.

After removing the deckle, a pulp sheet remains on the papermaking screen.

✳ Layering With Strips

Strips can be torn or pulled from a sheet with the help of a ruler and layered on a mold or matrix. They can be laid across the mold, each slightly overlapping the preceding one, until the mold is covered. A second layer can be added on at right angles to the first. Strips are an excellent way to build up a paper casting's thickness.

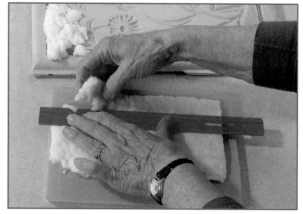

Using a ruler to tear strips from a pulp sheet.

✳ Making Sheets, Strips, and Shapes Without a Hand Mold

You will use this method for many of the projects in this book.

You Will Need

2 12-inch lengths of 1- by 2-inch (or larger) board
18-inch square piece of fine mesh hardware cloth and window screen
Bucket or tub
Plastic pitcher or turkey baster
Sponge, terrycloth, and/or paper towels

1 Put the hardware screen over the bucket.

2 Place the window screen over the hardware cloth.

3 Place two boards beside each other on the screen, as far apart as you want the strip or sheet to be wide.

4 Pour pulp from the pitcher slowly onto the screen between the boards, to whatever depth desired, or use a turkey baster to fill area between boards with pulp.

5 After the pulp has drained, remove the boards.

6 With a sponge, terrycloth, or paper toweling, de-water the strips or sheets to a point where they can be handled and applied to a surface.

Open ends exist at the ends of the boards. If desired, these can be blocked off with other boards or any suitable obstacle. Similarly, space between boards can be shortened lengthwise by placing blocks between them. Different length boards can be arranged to form different-shaped areas on the screen. A wedge shape (handy for making paper casts of bowls) can be made by moving the two ends of the boards closer together than the opposite two ends.

A wedge-shaped piece can be used to make a bowl.

✳ Pouring

For larger molds, pulp of a proper consistency can be poured directly onto the mold. This requires building a frame (sides) around the mold so the pulp does not run off. There is a thorough discussion and pictures of this method in Chapter 8, Casting on a Large Mold (page 80).

2

3

4

Chapter Five

Paper Casting With Everyday Objects

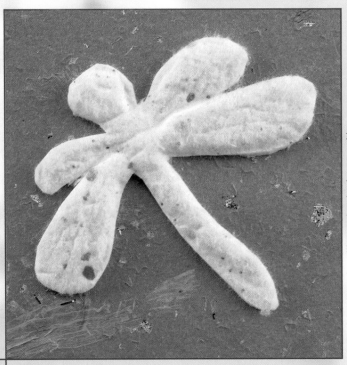

Cast paper made with crushed mica sparkles.

Chapter

5

"Everyday objects" is a limitless world in which your imagination can roam endlessly, and your decorative and artistic senses can find a thousand paths to pursue. There are certainly some everyday things around the house or maybe your grandmother's attic that can be used for paper casting.

Keep an eye on the amazing and functional shapes and forms found in fast food restaurants, ice cream parlors, and grocery stores. There are neat tray and small-box forms everywhere. Also, a round shape is universally pleasing, and can be useful as well.

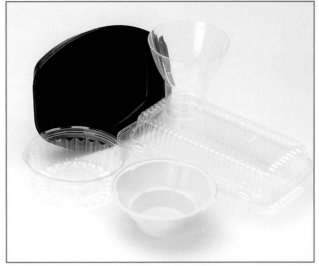

Various plastic forms...

Set a glass or similar round object in the middle of a larger round pulp patty. With a plastic spatula, push the pulp patty's edges up around the bottom of the matrix, let the pulp dry, and you get all types of coaster-like creations (see page 30). Spray them with clear acrylic and they will develop moisture resistance. You can also do your own thing freehand with a turkey baster as a drawing or forming tool.

Through surface embedment, you can celebrate and immortalize contemporary entertainment and commercial icons, a memento from your kid's card games, or the graduation card of a grandchild.

And the resulting paper casts.

Immortalize a cultural icon!

Tray with grandchild's graduation card.

And don't overlook the amazing versatility of simple pieces of wood, which can be cut to any size. As with the round objects mentioned on the previous page, wood pieces can be placed in the center of a larger, similarly shaped pulp patty. Pushing the pulp edges up around the wood piece can create a whole world of photo frames, knickknack trays and holders, frames for calligraphy, and so on.

Our everyday world is populated by hundreds of droll or exciting forms. Notice them. Any form that can support being covered with pulp, withstand damage from a release agent, as well as prolonged exposure to dampness, can be a paper casting matrix. This limitless selection can result in castings that are simply decorative, or that are marvelously handy and useful, as well as a pleasant blip on our everyday visual screen. As seen below, many shapes and forms can be found among plastic containers. Candidate matrices are everywhere. Search them out.

The one limiting factor is the "undercut." A casting has to be lifted from, or slid off of, the mold or matrix on which the pulp was laid. Therefore, any type of ledge, protrusion, or dimension that curls back under, which would prevent lifting or sliding of the dry casting from or off of the mold or matrix, is taboo. Beware of the undercut!

Ready to try paper casting? Let's get started!

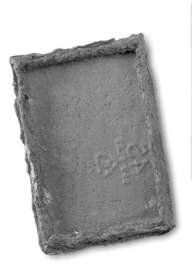

You can make interesting casts with an ordinary piece of wood.

Create a void in a casting to display a photo.

Matrices and the resulting casts.

Pulp pushed up around a glass set in the middle of a pulp patty.

Pulp pushed up around the edges of a wood block. Pulp was removed to make a photo frame.

Pulp simply poured around a round matrix, left, and a diamond-shaped matrix, above.

Tray with a child's playing card embedded in it.

Pulp pushed up around the edges of a wood block.

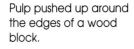

Free-hand poured pulp with the edge of a spatula.

Use an ordinary drinking glass or other round matrix to make coasters.

Functional paper castings for decoration and use on desk tops or night stands. The example at far right was made from a recycled church worship service bulletin.

Plastic deli containers can be used to make functional casts.

Use these practical shapes for holding pencils, pens,
paperclips, and other office supplies.

Cast Paper Tray

You Will Need

Matrix*
Pulp (cotton linters or waste paper), various
    colors
Blender
Release agent
Hardware cloth
Bucket or tub
Water
Window screen
2 small-dimension boards
Turkey baster
Sponge, terrycloth towel, and/or paper towel
Scissors
Toothbrush or larger firm-bristle brush
Thin-bladed knife

*For the first effort, keep it simple, like a smaller item with un-
complicated straight lines. This will get you in touch with pulp
(how it feels and acts). It will lead you into larger and more detailed matrices later.

1 Make pulp. Plain and simple doesn't have
to be uninviting and drab; use several colors of pulp, if you wish. **Note:** For recycling,
use a blender and an amount of paper that
would cover your matrix to three or four
thicknesses. The directions below use three
colors of recycled pulp.

2 Put release agent all over the surface of
the matrix.

3 Pick a method for applying pulp (such
as batch, strip, patty). For the matrix
shown here, strips work well.

4 Make pulp strips to lay over the matrix.
Lay the hardware cloth over the bucket
or tub into which water can drain. Put the
window screen on the hardware cloth (see
page 25). Lay the small-dimension boards beside each other on the window screen. Leave
as much distance between the boards as you
want the strips to be wide.

5 Take a turkey baster and put down pulp
between the boards, forming pulp strips.

6 By pressing with a sponge, terrycloth,
and/or paper towel, remove enough
water from the pulp strip so that it can be
lifted and handled.

1

4

5

7 Lay the strips over the matrix, entirely covering the surface.

8 To finish covering it, wrap an appropriate sized strip around each end. Cut the strips at the corners of the matrix. Fold the corners down and the middle part over them.

9 Put some finishing touches on the pulp surface. With a toothbrush or larger firm-bristle brush, pat all pulp edges to blend and blur them. Apply a bit of moisture, if necessary. With the brush, pat any other rough or uneven surfaces.

10 De-water the pulp by pressing it with a sponge, and then with terrycloth and/or paper toweling. Remove as much water as possible.

11 Dry the casting. A casting of this size and nature can be set in any optimum drying environment: in sunshine; next to or over a heat source; in an oven that has a bulb or pilot light, etc.

12 When completely dry, work (push or pull) the casting loose from the matrix. If necessary, insert a fingernail or thin-bladed knife under an edge to aid release. Do not try removal until the casting is totally dry.

And there you have it—your own, very first paper casting. You have *created*. Let it be just the first of many that continue to get bigger, better, and more amazing! Larger and more imposing paper casts are simply an extension of what you have just done. They will require a bigger matrix, more pulp, perhaps a variety of methods for applying pulp (strips, patties, circles, batches, etc.) to fit particular areas on the larger matrix, more water removal effort and drying time, and, above all, more patience. But it is fun!

7

8

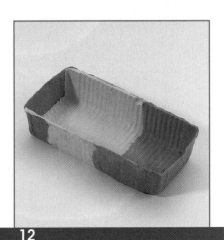

9

10

12

✳ Texture

Texture will be a part of most castings, often as surface detail; however, one can make textural detail the main feature of a paper casting. And rather than the texture being fine and subtle, it might be vigorous and obvious. One example is the following project.

Project Textured Cast Paper

Here, you will use a brick wall to create texture on the pulp; however, the possibilities are endless for textured cast paper. Use the instructions to pick up subtle textures from such everyday items as shelving liner, raised vinyl tablecloths, cloth like burlap, scrub boards, corrugated plastic, and even your house!

When you are done creating your textured piece, use it for collage, picture frames, cards, or scrapbook page layouts—or just frame it.

You Will Need

Pulp
Pour hand mold equipment (see page 24)
Brick wall
Sponge, terrycloth towel, and/or paper towel
Water

1 For application to a wall, pour pulp into the form of a single thick sheet. Here, we used an 8-1/2- by 11-inch pour hand mold, which places a deckle over a screen. Pulp is poured into the deckle, forming a sheet on the screen (see page 24).

2 Apply pulp to the brick wall (or other surface with a similarly gross texture). **Note:** It is possible that bricks might have undercuts. Close examination of the brick surface should be done prior to pulp application.

3 Remove as much water as possible with sponge, terrycloth towel, and/or paper toweling. Let dry.

4 When totally dry, carefully release from wall and admire.

1

2

3

✳ Cookie Cutters

The rabbit illustration used later in Arranging Solid Color Areas on page 56 introduces a whole world of ready-made, easily available, and often very attractive matrices for paper castings. A stylized cookie cutter, the rabbit is representative of a broad world of art on cookie cutter racks. The fare ranges from primitive folk to sophisticatedly stylized. It's a great world in which to do color casting experiments, develop color skill, and create all types of lovely things people will buy or cherish as gifts— or just use it for therapy. It is a varied and valuable resource on the craft level. Become a happy hunter!

Closed, or solid surface, cookie cutter.

Open cookie cutter.

Two types of cookie cutters are available: an image in the form of a simple open-ended frame and an image in the form of a solid surface on which is a raised pattern of ridges.

Open Cookie Cutters

With open cookie cutters, a single pulp color can be used to fill the entire image area, or different colored pulp segments can be placed next to each other. Directions for using this type of cookie cutter are given on the following page.

A personalized equivalent of the open cookie cutter can easily be made by first drawing an outline image of your favorite tree, animal, or even a profile of yourself or a friend, on foam board or any similar material. Next, with a "hot wire" (available at art stores) or thin sharp knife, cut out the image. This is truly personalized; the possibilities are endless!

Personalized foam board outlines.

Open Cookie Cutters and Personalized Matrices

Open cookie cutters and personalized foam board matrices are used in exactly the same way. The following directions show a personalized foam board matrix.

You Will Need

Foam board cut-out or open cookie cutter
Bucket
Screen
Pulp, colored
Sponge, terrycloth towel, and/or paper towel

1 Put foam board with a cutout matrix on a screen surface so water can drain (see page 25).

2 With a turkey baster or by hand, put colored pulps at selected areas inside the matrix, according to the desired pattern.

3 Remove water with sponge, terrycloth towel, and/or paper towel. Let dry.

4 Lift away foam board.

The finished, dry casting.

Note that wet colored pulp is much brighter and more vivid than when it is dry.

1

2

Solid Surface Cookie Cutters

Because these molds have a solid bottom, no drainage surface is needed. The following explains how to use them.

You Will Need

Solid surface (closed) cookie cutter
Release agent
Pulp, colored
Sponge, terrycloth towel, and/or paper towel
Turkey baster

1 Put release agent on cookie cutter.

2 With turkey baster or fingers, put different colors of pulp in "fenced off" areas.

3 Press water out of each color as you put it down, until it is level with, or below, the ridge tops. Clean up any pulp that has spilled out of its area.

4 When color areas have been placed, put a reasonably substantial, continuous layer of pulp over all of them.

5 Remove as much water as possible with a sponge, terrycloth towel, and/or paper toweling.

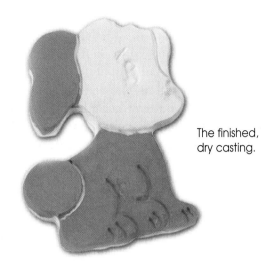

The finished, dry casting.

6 Let the casting dry.

7 Release casting from cookie cutter.

Solid surface cookie cutter.

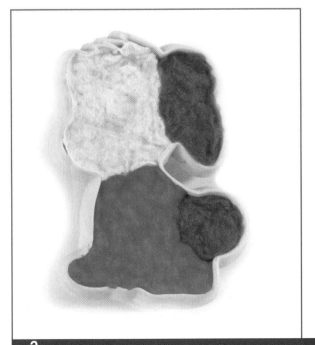

2

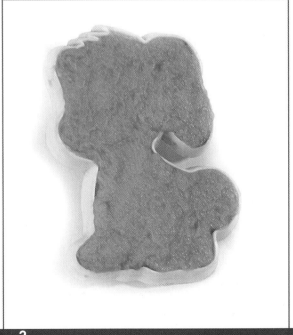

3

In any multi-color casting, a weak spot exists where one colored pulp meets another; fiber batches do not bond strongly where they touch. Consequently, a substantial continuous pulp layer over the casting's back is necessary to hold the dried casting together. The following will also help:

• Slightly overlap each color.
• Color "joints" can be wetted and the edges "teased" together with a pin or soft brush, or patted with the bristles of a toothbrush.
• Place a continuous layer of pulp over all colors at the end of color placement to prevent the dried paper casting from breaking at color joints.

Here are some other solutions:

• Wet the joints and "tease" the colors together with the point of a pin. Wetting gives fibers some mobility.

• Hit a "joint" from either side with a stream of water from a spray bottle. This must be handled deftly and with a delicate touch or irreparable harm can occur.
• Wet the joints and pat them with the bristles of a toothbrush.

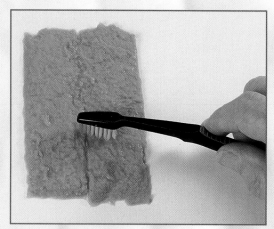

Patting joints with a toothbrush.

A lovely summer scene.

Make all of the animals on Old MacDonald's farm!

Make a cow to jump over these moons! We used colored fibers for the eyes and mouths.

Christmas in Sherwood Forest... individual cookie cutter casts, each glued to a penny to stand up. Colored details were added with colored pulp dipped on a pin.

Fun Christmas ornaments and figures to adorn your tree and tabletop.

Chapter Six

Paper Pottery: Paper-cast Bowls

Chapter

6

Cast paper finished with watercolor pencil and glitter pen by Debra S. Beagle.

nyone can make a simple paper-cast bowl immediately! The bowl can be made by simply pouring a slurry of pulp into a kitchen strainer and letting it drain and dry. With a little more effort and time, it is possible to make a more complex bowl. This chapter presents two methods for making a paper-cast bowl. The first is forming it with a kitchen strainer as the matrix, while the second is placing wet pulp on the solid surface of a bowl or bowl form.

A simple bowl.

A more complex "rigged" bowl.

Further, many different, and very diverse, kinds of paper-cast bowls can be made by simply exercising a choice of which waste paper to recycle into pulp for the castings. Both of the bowls below are made of pulp obtained by recycling very ordinary paper present in most homes. The one on the left is recycled wrapping paper, and the one on the right is recycled food packaging.

The variations, personal practices, and ultimate nuances of bowl making are legion. This book's aim is to present the unchanging basics common to all of them. Knowing the basics lets you climb as high into the realms of craft and art (or commercial success) as your particular talent, imagination, and industry can take you. But it is time for hands-on…

Paper-cast bowls made of recycled waste paper.

Easy Bowl With an Everyday Kitchen Strainer

Perhaps the easiest, and certainly the fastest, way to make a paper-cast bowl is to pour liquid pulp into a kitchen strainer up to the brim, let it drain, and dry. What kind of bowl you get will be decided by nature, what kind of strainer you used, what kind of pulp you poured, how liquid (dilute) the pulp was, and so forth, but regardless of these things, you will get a bowl!

A variety of strainers,

You Will Need

Kitchen strainer, round
Blender
Sponge, terrycloth towel, and/or paper towel
Pulp: new cotton linters or recycled selected
    white or colored waste paper
Sink or screen over bucket
Plastic pitcher
8-ounce glass
Turkey baster

1 Place the kitchen strainer over a sink or a screen over bucket (see page 25).

2 With a blender, make pulp, using either cotton linters or waste paper (see pages 10 and 14).

3 Save some pulp for later touch-up work (approximately an 8-ounce glass full).

4 Pour the remainder of the wet pulp into the kitchen strainer. Pour quickly and continuously until all pulp has been poured. **Note:** This will likely fill the strainer to the top, which is good. Should the strainer overflow, stop pouring briefly, then pour the remainder.

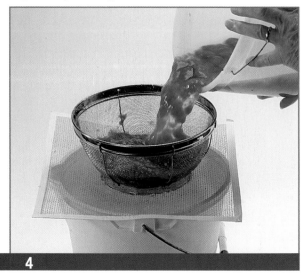

4

Making Pulp

For cotton linters, put the amount of linters according to the package directions into water in a blender and run until dispersed. If no specific amount is directed, make an estimate (experiment; run a given amount of linters in the blender and see how much of the bowl's surface it covers, then figure out how much is needed for the entire bowl).

For white or colored recycled paper:

- Tear up the equivalent of two and a half standard sheets of paper (8-1/2- by 11-inch sheets) and put them in a blender nearly filled with water.
- Run the blender on a high speed for 30 seconds, then pour the pulp into a container.
- Repeat the process two more times. This will give you sufficient pulp for a 7- to 8-inch diameter strainer.
- For your first effort, consider using a brown or white grocery sack. Because either has a good, long fiber, soak for an hour before dispersing in the blender.

5 Let the pulp drain completely until all excess water has gone, and the pulp has set firmly in the strainer. **Note:** Depending on the pulp and type of strainer, the pulp might be left deposited unevenly on the strainer's sides. Should this occur, get the pulp that was saved in Step 3. With a turkey baster, take the pulp and deposit it where necessary to achieve even distribution on the sides. This procedure can also be used to straighten the rim.

6 When the pulp has set firmly, lift the strainer and hold its sides to a light source (light will be transmitted through the pulp). Where the light is very bright, the pulp wall is the thinnest. Note where the thin spots are. Use a turkey baster and "saved" pulp from Step 3 to reinforce weak spots, as described in Step 5.

Continued on the next page.

5

6

7 Start removing water by pressing a sponge around the outside of the strainer's sides and bottom. Continue until the sponge no longer removes water. Repeat the process directly on the pulp inside the strainer. Follow on the inside with terrycloth and paper toweling. (Do not throw the wet/damp paper away; let it dry and use it for your next project.)

8 Place the strainer where the pulp will dry fastest (in the sun, in moving air, next to a register, in oven with a pilot light, etc.). **Note:** A hair dryer or room heater can be used, but if the heat is too great or the exposure too long, the pulp might become discolored.

9 Let the bowl dry completely. It must be absolutely dry or it might crack during the removal procedure. If in doubt, wait.

10 Starting with your fingers and thumb pressing onto the outside of the strainer, very carefully work the bowl loose and remove it from strainer. Remember, unless totally dry, the bowl will crack during removal operations. If bowl removal is generally unsuccessful, make your next bowl thicker by using more pulp; see page 46 for ways to make bowl walls thicker—and therefore stronger.

7

10

And there you have your "pour" bowl. It is light, substantial, and a new shape on your scene. Further decoration by whatever medium you choose can be applied, or simply put some real, or faux, fruit in it and put it on your table as a recurring reminder that you, too, are a creator!

A white (instead of brown) grocery sack would have produced the paper-cast bowl shown at left. If you had poured two colors of pulp into the strainer, one color on each side simultaneously, instead of just one color, you would have made a two-color bowl something like the two below.

Bowl made from a white grocery sack.

Bowl made from two colors of pulp poured at once.

Bowl Removal

Pulp fibers, during pouring, squeeze into the strainer's openings. They can hang there tenaciously, complicating bowl removal. Above all, employ care and patience. Try as follows:

- With fingers and thumb, press in on the strainer sides. Don't worry about deforming the strainer; it can be pushed back into shape later. Start pressing gently, then press harder. Start at the top, all of the way around, then press gradually lower on the sides. Repeat at and near the top until the bowl pops loose (one area at a time) from the strainer. Continue circular pressing until the bowl's sides pop loose entirely.

- Repeat the procedure on the screen's bottom. Normally, the bottom has more pulp penetration into the screen openings and requires more and harder pressing. Eventually, the bowl might have to be literally pulled loose from strainer bottom. Above all, use your eyes and simple good sense in the removal procedure. If you see something bad happening, press elsewhere.

Controlling How Much Pulp Goes Where When Making a Strainer-cast Bowl

If you want a bowl's walls to be thicker for appearance or strength, try either of the following:

1 While the pulp is draining, tip the strainer a bit to one side. Dip a wide spatula into the strainer and move pulp up and onto the strainer's sides.

2 Pour pulp directly onto the strainer's sides instead of onto its bottom. Place the strainer on its side. Put the spout of the pulp container down as low and close to the strainer as possible. Pour pulp slowly as a thick slurry. After the poured pulp has set, roll the strainer back and pour again. Be sure each pour overlaps the previous. If the pulp is thick enough and the strainer is rolled slowly enough, it might be possible to pour pulp and roll the strainer on its sides at the same time. But the pulp must be given sufficient time to set as, or before, the strainer is rolled, or it will fall back off of the strainer's sides.

1

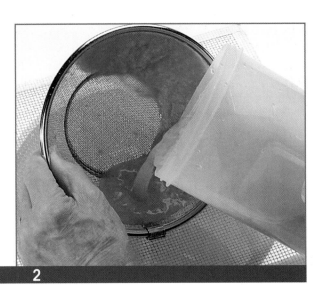

2

Would you like a colored rim on your paper-cast bowl? When the pulp has drained, tilt the strainer on its side. With a turkey baster, deposit a colored pulp all of the way around the bowl at the edge of its rim. Continue with regular water removal and drying.

Making a Solid-surface Cast Bowl or Bowl Shape

Putting pulp on the inner or outer surface of a solid bowl or bowl shape and letting it dry will make a paper-cast bowl. How pulp is applied affects the bowl's final appearance (see Chapter 4).

Common to any pulp application method are the need to de-water the pulp enough that it can be handled for placement, and the need to have each pulp placement somewhat overlap the preceding one so that there are no voids in the coverage and all pulp bonds. (See Step 6 for information about blurring and blending edges of overlap patties.)

You Will Need

Bowl
Pulp
Blender
Release agent
Turkey baster
Equipment needed to make wedge-shaped
    patties (see page 25)
Sponge, terrycloth towel, and/or paper towel
Plastic spatula or firm-bristle brush
Thin-bladed knife

1 Select a bowl or bowl shape of which the casting is to be made. For your first effort, pick something on the small side and with simple lines. This will let you get to know pulp, how it handles, and its general personality. Handling smaller pieces of wet pulp first will give you knowledge and experience to handle larger ones later.

2 Apply the release agent to bowl surface (inner or outer) on which pulp is to be placed.

3 Prepare new pulp, or recycle selected paper, in a blender (see pages 10 and 14).

4 Decide which application method to use. Because bowls are generally bigger at the top than the bottom, it is good to apply pulp in wedge-shaped patties. These can be made with a turkey baster and two lengths of board as shown on page 25, but with the boards arranged to make a wedge-shaped area.

Continued on the next page.

2

4

5 With a sponge, terrycloth, and paper toweling, dry the wedge-shaped patty sufficiently that it can be handled. Pick it up and apply it to the bowl's surface.

6 Blur and smooth the overlapped edges. **Note:** When a strip in any shape is overlapped, the strip's edge is a "ridge" on the surface. It is desirable to blur the edge, blending and smoothing it into the adjacent surface. This can be done by simply pushing it down with your thumb or fingers, blurring it by brushing with a plastic spatula, or by wetting the edge and patting it with a firm-bristled brush.

7 Continue making and applying wedge-shaped patties, each slightly overlapping the previous one, and finishing the bottom with additional pulp if needed, until the entire bowl surface is covered.

8 Remove water. Press the pulp-covered bowl between your hands, each holding a sponge. Go entirely around the bowl and the bottom. Wring the sponges after each press.

9 Set the bowl in a good drying place, or place in the oven (not microwave) at minimum heat. Let dry completely.

10 Carefully work the paper casting free from the matrix bowl. This might require repeated firm to gentle urging. Work a thumbnail or thin-bladed knife under the casting's upper edge, if necessary and possible, and work from there. If a proper release agent has been adequately applied, release should occur.

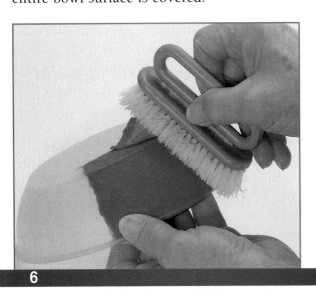

6

7

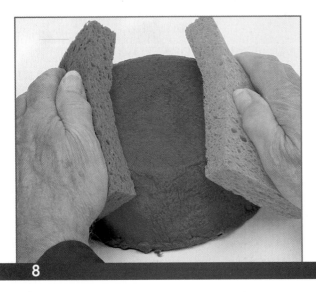

8

10

Here is another bowl being covered with wedge-shaped patties; it will be a "desert colors" bowl. Note how the edges of the overlapped patties have been blended into each other.

You, too, can learn how to "paint" pictures on pulp patties for one-of-a-kind bowls (see page 53 for information).

Interesting shaped bowl made with a variety of colored patties.

Consider signing your paper-cast bowl in pulp. Dip a long pin into thick pulp; the pin will pick up pulp on its barrel. Drag the pin along the surface of the wet pulp, causing the pulp to slide off of the barrel in a line. It takes time, but it is a great touch.

Chapter Seven

Enhancing Paper Casts

Cast paper finished with watercolor pencil by Debra S. Beagle.

Chapter

7

olor is always a favorite enhancement. Casting with color requires pulps of different colors (regular fibers that have been dyed).

How to Get Colored Pulps

The easiest, least expensive, and fastest way to get colored pulp is to disperse the dyed fibers that make up colored paper, which is recycling in a blender.

Does this provide good colored pulp? Our opinion is that it provides the best colored pulp! Fibers making up colored paper have been dyed at pulp or paper mills by experienced professionals using the best dyes, the best equipment, at the right temperatures, under monitoring by state-of-the-art instruments, to meet the unyielding demands of the commercial design and graphic arts worlds. This is hard to match at home; however, wanting to do one's own thing certainly is fine, and sometimes something short of technical quality can be a desirable effect.

If you want to make your own colored pulp, get papermaking dyes from a reputable vendor (see page 95). If you want to be even more basic, there are books available at your local library or bookstore that are partially or totally about dyeing with a variety of plants and plant parts. In the end, if you want colored pulps mostly free and now, select good colored papers from the waste stream (remember—waste paper is not waste fiber) and turn them back into pulp by recycling.

For pure color, cut away all parts of the paper that have been printed upon, or go to an office supply or paper specialty store. Especially at the latter, you will find colors, hues, and tints you have never dreamed of. Many of the papers will be permanent.

Put the papers in a blender with water (about 3 cups with an 8-1/2- by 11-inch sheet). Run the blender for 20 to 30 seconds. You will have in your blender the same colored pulp that the paper mill put on its paper machine to make the paper you recycled. Use inexpensive paper, such as construction paper, with caution. The dye generally is so loose that even a snippet of the paper will color everything in sight. Some people use just a little construction paper in the blender with white paper to make dyed pulp.

Pursue any path to colored pulp that your time, interest-level, and talent indicate; that's part of the excitement of the craft and art world. The following are some basic ways to put color into a paper casting.

"Waste" paper can be recycled into colored pulp.

✳ Putting Color in Before Pulp Is Applied

Here are numerous ways to color pulp.

Solid Colors

Make successive pulp patties, sheets, or strips of different colors. Apply them to a mold's or matrix's surface.

Add Color

Mix and/or insert color into or on a pulp patty. To do this, make a pulp patty, leaving it as wet as possible. If necessary, spray it to re-wet. Add color by pouring colored pulp onto the patty's surface and mixing/kneading the color into patty's surface. As shown below, put color in more controlled form on the patty's surface with a turkey baster. Re-flatten the patty as necessary and apply to the matrix's surface.

Solid colored strips.

Flow-together Color Strips

Make a patty on a screen or sieve surface by pouring, or putting down with a turkey baster, side-by-side strips of different colored pulps. If pulp is kept thin enough, pulp strips will flow together and bond strongly. Apply the patty to the surface.

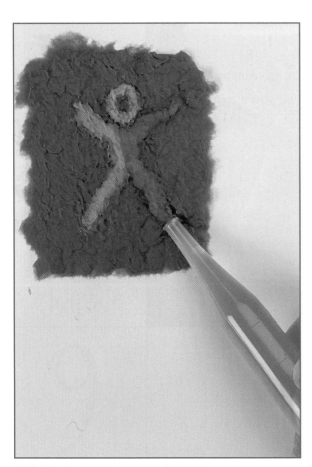

Applying pulp carefully with a turkey baster.

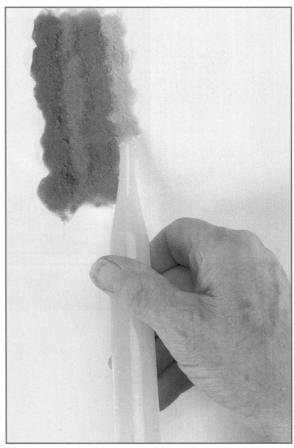

Different colored pulp strips laid side-by-side create a unique patty.

Colored Pulp Substitution

Make a patty, leaving it as wet as possible. Place an open cookie cutter, or a shape cut out of foam board or similar material, on the patty's surface. Holding the shape firmly down upon the pulp surface, use your fingers or tweezers to remove all of the pulp within the shape. By pouring, or with a turkey baster, fill in the shape with different colored pulp. Apply to the surface of a matrix.

Pulp Painting: Specific Image

To paint pulp, first make a pulp patty, removing as little water as possible. Put a piece of fine hardware cloth over a bucket. Put a piece of window screen over the hardware cloth; this provides a surface on which to do a pulp painting. Put an image on the window screen; it can be a favorite cookie cutter or your own image cut out of foam board or a similar material. Fill the image with one or more colors by pouring or with a turkey baster. This creates a single or multi-colored image on the screen.

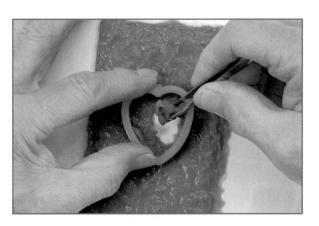

Use a tweezers to remove pulp.

The ideal surface for pulp painting.

Fill in the open area with a different color of pulp.

Fill in the open area with pulp.

The results can be quite dramatic!

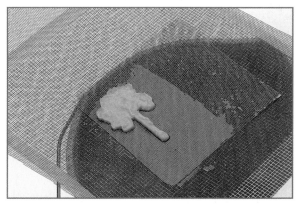

This tree will make a great addition to a unique bowl or can stand in its own.

Pulp Painting: Abstract Image

By pouring different colored pulps onto the surface of the screen, or simply squirting them on randomly with a turkey baster (on top of or beside each other), you can create colorful abstract images.

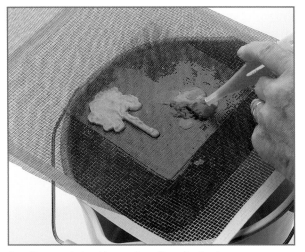

Creating an abstract image is really quite simple.

Putting Pulp Paintings on a Pulp Surface

When completed on a screen, paintings can be transferred to a pulp surface. First, lift the screen with the image on it. Turn it upside down so the pulp image is on the bottom. Lower the pulp image down onto the surface of the pulp patty made above. Now press a sponge on the area of the screen over the painting. This will transfer the painting from the screen to the pulp's surface. Slowly and carefully lift the screen, leaving the painting on the pulp's surface.

Transferring the painting to a patty's surface.

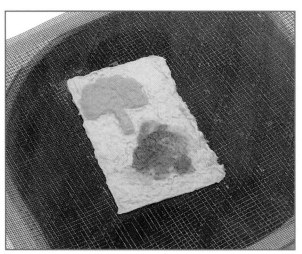

The patty is ready to be applied to a matrix surface, or it would make a great greeting card.

These three strainer bowls bear pulp paintings. At left is the specific image of a heart; at right is an abstract on a bowl's interior bottom; and in the middle is a "picture."

Veining

Veining can make a very dramatic statement on a paper cast item. To do this, shoot the surface of a pulp patty with a jet stream of colored pulp as follows: Make a pulp patty, leaving it as wet as possible. Put very dilute-colored pulp into a small plastic squeezable container which has, or can be fitted with, a cap with a very small nozzle hole. Aim the nozzle at the patty's surface and squeeze, shooting a jet stream of pulp onto the patty's surface. While squeezing, keep the jet stream moving across the patty's surface.

This will leave a colored trail across the patty's surface. Moving the aim and the squeezing action must be coordinated. If the movement is too slow, the jet stream will simply blast a hole in the pulp patty's surface. If it is too fast, no color will be left in the track. Small nozzle holes might frequently plug up. If so, make pulp more dilute, or if the nozzle is clogged, it can be unplugged with a pin. Finally, apply the patty to the surface of a matrix.

At left is a strainer bowl to which veining was done after pulp had drained in the strainer. For the solid surface bowl at right, veining was done to pulp patties, which were then applied to the bowl's surface.

Spray a jet stream of pulp onto the patty's surface for a beautiful veined look.

The finished veined piece.

The preceding techniques, with the possible exception of veining (which can be used with paper-cast bowls made with strainers) can also be used to put color onto pulp after it has been applied to mold or bowl surfaces. The possible variations and combinations of the above techniques are near infinite. (For a detailed look at color art and decorative techniques, see Arnold Grummer's Complete Guide to Easy Papermaking.)

✳ Arranging Solid Color Areas

Colored pulp can be placed anywhere on the surfaces of flat molds or dimensional forms. It simply requires choosing a good method of placing it (pin, tweezers, fingers, pieces, batch, pouring, turkey baster, etc.) and a bit of care. Experience will bring you greater skill. The process is simple: decide where you want which color, get the colored pulp desired, and put it where you want it, as shown below with an open cookie cutter.

This casting could have been applied to a wet bowl's surface as a pulp painting, but was left in this instance to dry as a separate independent paper casting. See more about use of cookie cutters on page 35.

Apply different colored pulp in the open area with care!

Color placement is complete.

For the paper casting at left, color areas were put on solid surface bowl as individual batches. For the vase at right, color areas were applied as strips.

You can trim any jagged or uneven edges of a dried paper casting with ordinary or decorative-edge scissors.

Flat Molds

Colored pulp can be put on areas as wet globs, patties, or squeezed out of a turkey baster. It then needs to be confined to the selected area. Its edges can be pushed into place and clearly established with a plastic spatula or similar object.

Removing some water after the pulp is placed will help stabilize it as adjacent pulp colors are placed. Color placement is totally stabilized when the casting's final coat of white pulp has been applied and the casting has dried.

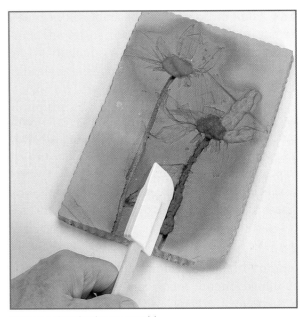

Placing colored pulps on a mold.

A backing of white pulp was placed over the colored pulp, resulting in this finished color casting.

Putting Botanicals in Paper Castings

Plants, either whole or parts of, can be put in or on paper castings. It is assumed most, if not all, botanical addition will be only to paper-cast bowls and other forms, and not to flat commercial molds.

Ferns are ideal for use with paper pulp. They are visually pleasing, somewhat delicate, and their structure catches pulp fibers, which results in firm bonding (tying) to a pulp surface. Leaves, petals, grass, small flowers, clover, and so forth all fare fairly well in the paper pulp environment.

When used in hand papermaking or paper casting, botanicals are exposed to water and dampness for varying periods of time. The water can leech color out of the botanicals and into adjacent fibers, which can create a color corona around the botanical. Some botanicals turn totally black, which can be pleasing—or displeasing.

Botanicals are probably handled best with the whole-sheet method of applying pulp.

When pulp containing botanicals is poured into a hand mold to create a sheet or into a strainer to create a bowl, the botanicals tend to rise to the surface as the pulp drains. This puts most botanical elements on one side of the sheet and therefore the subsequent bowl.

Botanicals can be put in whole, partially, or completely shredded. To shred, place botanicals in the blender when paper (recycling) or new pulp is dispersed by water into liquid pulp. To shred into small parts, place botanicals in at the beginning. To shred only slightly, put botanicals in when paper or dry pulp has been almost completely dispersed into liquid pulp. To place small, whole botanicals, put them in liquid pulp after the blender operation.

Any of the above is called *internal* embedment. The botanical elements will be literally a part of the pulp, though some will indeed be visible externally on the casting's surface. However, external placement is done by "surface embedment"; it places botanicals (as well as other materials) directly on the surface. In internal embedment, botanicals are placed randomly by nature, while in surface embedment, they can be placed at a specific location.

A variety of botanicals can enhance your paper-cast projects.

Applying Botanicals: Internal Embedment

Here are some easy instructions for embedding botanicals into pulp.

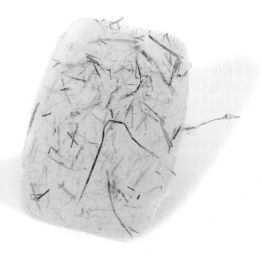

The bowl at left has flower petals embedded into it, while the tray at right has ordinary lawn grass.

You Will Need

Botanicals
Pulp
Blender
Strainer

1 Put the botanicals in the blender for full or partial shredding, or place whole botanicals into liquid pulp after the blender process.

2 Pour pulp into the strainer and apply directly to the matrix surface, or make pulp patties for application to the surface.

Botanicals Can Be Added...

- In the blender any time during pulp making.
- Into liquid pulp after the blender process.
- On the surface, embedded on wet pulp before or after pulp is applied to the casting matrix.

This sheet was made by placing whole botanicals from an old bouquet into liquid pulp after the blender process. The pulp was then poured into a deckle over a screen, forming the sheet (see page 24).

Applying Botanicals: Surface Embedment

If you would rather embed the botanicals on the surface of the pulp, follow these instructions. **Note:** *See Arnold Grummer's Complete Guide to Easy Papermaking* for more information and photos. The following steps show how to embed the botanical on a wet pulp surface, whether it is a sheet made with a hand mold, pulp patty, or a pulp covering already applied to a bowl or other matrix.

You Will Need

Botanicals
Pulp
Water
Turkey baster
Cup or glass
Equipment needed to make patties (see page 25)

1 Select botanical.

2 Make pulp (see page 10). Save some liquid pulp in a container.

3 Make a pulp patty, as shown on page 25.

4 Take pulp saved in Step 2 and add water to it (to make it thinner).

5 Dip the botanical into the saved pulp. This will deposit some pulp on the botan-

ical's edges and other parts. **Note:** If the botanical picks up so much pulp that some or much of the botanical is hidden, make the pulp thinner and re-dip. This is especially true of fine structures such as ferns and arbor vitae. Such things as oak leaves might pick up practically nothing; for these, see Step 7.

6 Lay botanical where desired on pulp surface.

5

6

7 If it appears that insufficient pulp has been caught on the botanical with dipping process, use a turkey baster and the saved pulp to dribble pulp over the botanical's edges and other parts. **Note:** Pulp on the edges or parts of a botanical must reach to the surface of the pulp on which botanical was placed. This ties botanical to pulp's surface.

8 If the botanical has been embedded on a pulp sheet or patty, it is ready to be applied to a bowl or other matrix surface.

Don't think only botanicals when thinking surface embedment. How about your favorite football player, TV personality, relative, or family member?

Make a paper casting that can be read.

Bowls and containers enhanced with embedded botanicals.

Project Botanicals Above a Bowl's Edge

Botanicals (as well as pennants and flags) can be made to rise out of a bowl's or matrix's wall and extend above the rim. This technique should engage many minds and imaginations in some quite fascinating undertakings.

You Will Need

Paper-cast bowl (see Chapter 6)
Pulp
Botanical with stem
Spatula or water in bottle

1 Complete placement of pulp on the inside of a bowl (including strainer) or any other suitable matrix. Save some of the pulp.

2 Assemble a real or artificial botanical with a bare stem. For a first effort, work with a small botanical.

3 Place the bare stem down along the inside of the bowl wall, vertically. The stem should extend an inch or more below the bowl rim. Hold it steady in place for next the step.

4 Take pulp leftover from Step 1, or different pulp of some complementary color, and lap it over the stem from the bottom up to the rim, thickly and well.

5 With your fingers, spatula, or light spray of water, blend pulp around the stem into and with the bowl wall's pulp.

6 Let the paper casting dry.

4

5

Obviously, botanicals for this technique cannot be too big or bulky. Anything physically suitable, other than botanicals, can also be embedded (see the bowl with handle on this book's cover). This technique can be used with any paper casting matrix that has suitable wall structure.

More ideas to try!

✳ Glitter and Glisten

A wide range of products can add a special spark to your paper-cast projects.

Sparkle, lights, and a touch of elegance can adorn your castings, especially those designed for, and hung on, a Christmas tree. A broad and varied selection of light-reflecting agents can be added to casting pulps. All can be added in the blender for some modification of particle size, or in the pulp after the blender to keep them in their original size. Addition in various amounts can produce effects ranging from an accent to a visual assault.

Glitter and glisten agents include micalites, opalites, crystalites, and ultrafine glitters. Broad selections can be found in craft stores, and a varied selection has been developed by vendor Greg Markim, Inc.

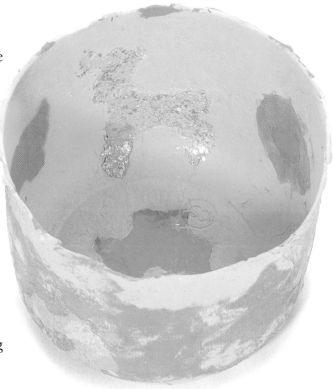

A glitter and glisten deer is a pulp painting on the inside of this solid surface paper-cast bowl.

A stunning array of glitter and glisten ornaments.

✳ Mottling

Mottling can have an impressive effect on bowls. To do this, put either numerous colors of paper or paper covered with many brilliant inks into the blender. Turn the blender off while there are still pieces of whole paper (before all of the fibers come apart when recycling paper into pulp). Make a paper cast either with a strainer or of a solid surface bowl.

A mottled bowl with solid colored stripes.

Turning a blender off early when recycling paper into pulp can create a beautiful mottled effect, as shown by these bowls.

Chapter Eight

Making and Using Your Own Molds

Cast paper highlighted with a glitter glue pen by Debra S. Beagle.

Chapter

8

igid molds can be formed using a commercial hard plaster or cement; this book will call mold making products the "mold medium." Each has different properties and advantages. The choice of a medium might depend on what is available in the nearest art, hobby, or craft store, but the Internet provides additional options.

The chosen medium will be prepared and then poured over the model (object) of which a mold is to be made. Or, when using a small model, such as a button or a shell, the model can be embedded into the poured medium.

The model should be something that can be visualized as a lovely paper casting when left white or finished with spray paints or other media (see Surface Decoration, page 20). Examples in this book might spark the imagination to find or create something personally exciting and gratifying. It can be an item chosen from something used in everyday routine, purchased from an antique store or rummage sale, or from nature. After a brief discussion of release agents, we will present some considerations when choosing a model.

✳ Release Agents

Release of a casting from a mold, and release agents, were discussed earlier (see Chapter 3). Release is a concern when choosing a model from which to make a mold. A dimensional model must separate from the new mold without harm to either, and it must not have undercuts. Remember that undercuts are surface depressions, bulges, or "curl backs" that prevent the mold from being removed without breaking either the model or the mold.

From models of metal or plastic, release is generally easy. Application of the chosen release agent to the model before pouring the plaster should assure release after the plaster has hardened.

Stone, plaster, wood, or cement models must be sealed with a varnish, shellac, paste wax, or spray polyurethane, and then treated with a release agent that will work on the sealant. A clean separation assures that the mold and the model are not bonded to each other forever. If you are unsure about which sealant to use with a particular model, check with an expert at your favorite paint store.

The basic supplies needed for mold making.

✳ Mold Sizes

Cast paper projects range in size from less than an inch in diameter to huge wall-sized pieces. Creating a small rigid mold and a small finished paper casting is simple and easy. Difficulty increases as the size increases, and estimating amounts of casting medium and water for very large pieces is very difficult. After a large rigid mold is complete, other tasks begin: preparing large amounts of pulp, forming the wet pulp into layers on the mold, and removing water from the paper cast, which can mean hours of hard work. Drying a large paper cast requires care to keep it flat; however, the larger the size, the more spectacular and impressive the piece will be.

A wide variety of objects that can be used to create a mold; they range in size from a tiny button to a very large wood engraving.

✳ Depth of Relief or Dimension

Dimensional models vary in depth, or relief. Some will be nearly flat, only having indented or raised lines and spaces. Others will have extreme variations of surface. Again, the greater the differences of highs and lows in the model, the more care is needed when forming the mold. Yet, the choice should be pleasing, both from a challenging and aesthetic viewpoint. Check models for imperfections. Cracks and holes in the model will also appear in the mold and paper cast, but many can be repaired.

✳ Choosing the Medium to Make a Plaster Mold

Because mold making is not a common craft, only a few casting mediums can be found in art, hobby, or craft stores, but the Internet has many choices. Products that assure success have the following characteristics:

they are set very hard, strong, unaffected by exposure to watery pulp, and pick up the finest of details. Two products that have these qualities are Permastone and Hydrocal White Gypsum Cement; each will make a strong, hard mold. Being white, they assure that the finished mold will not color the finished casting, which is of special concern if bright white linters are being used. Note that plaster of Paris is not recommended as a mold-making medium.

✳ Let the Mold Making Begin!

For both mold making and paper casting, projects of different sizes call for differences of techniques. This chapter includes instructions for making molds and casts of different sizes. Directions for different casting mediums vary in the ratio of plaster to water, so remember that a mixed medium ready to pour should always have the consistency of mayonnaise or a milkshake. Follow the mixing directions on the mold medium being used.

Simple designs without undercuts and filigree are easy to work with. Notice repairs made with clay to fill in undercuts on the model on the right.

Project A Shell Mold...

This shell was chosen because it is a good beginning project—it is simple and beautiful. It has lovely lines with deep dimension and no undercuts. The release should come easily.

Materials

Shell
Small disposable cup
Mold medium
Water
Measuring spoons
Release agent (vegetable or silicone spray)
Paper toweling
Stick or plastic spoon
Rubber gloves

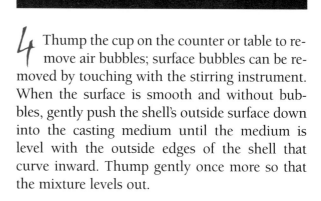

1 Spray the shell's outside surface with the chosen release agent. Wipe off any excess.

2 Measure 1 tablespoon and 2 teaspoons of water into the cup. Put the gloves on.

3 Measure 4 tablespoons of mold medium. Slowly sprinkle the mold medium into the water and let it be absorbed. Lightly stir until all of the plaster is dissolved. The desired mixture should have the look of mayonnaise or a milkshake. Additional water or mold medium should be added a small amount at a time, if needed. Again stir.

4 Thump the cup on the counter or table to remove air bubbles; surface bubbles can be removed by touching with the stirring instrument. When the surface is smooth and without bubbles, gently push the shell's outside surface down into the casting medium until the medium is level with the outside edges of the shell that curve inward. Thump gently once more so that the mixture levels out.

5 Put the cup aside, undisturbed, for at least 1 hour. During this hardening period, the cast will get warm and then cool again.

6 Clean utensils immediately; rinse off in a bowl of water. Do not wash mold medium

3

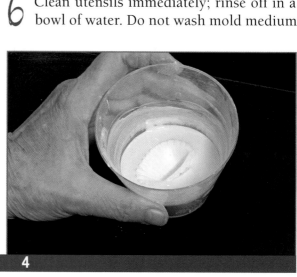

4

down the drain; dispose of water outdoors. When the mold is hard, peel or strip the cup away if it is paper. If it is plastic, the mold can be dropped from the cup. Separate the shell off of the mold. If a bubble formed in the mold under the shell and there is a hole there, the hole can be filled with a small amount of mold medium mixed with a tiny amount of water; apply to the hole with a flat toothpick.

7 Let the mold cure for a day before using. Wash it with clear water, spray it with a release agent when dry, and the mold is ready for making a cast.

Project ... A Paper-cast Shell

Now that the seashell mold has been created, let's use it. The mold is quite deep, but because it is small, the "pieces" method will be used to place the pulp.

You Will Need

Shell mold
Cotton linters
Water
Blender
Small strainer
Sponge, terrycloth towel, and/or paper towel

1 Prepare enough pulp to fill the mold by dispersing cotton linters in water in a blender (see pages 10 and 15).

2 Pour the pulp from the blender into a small strainer.

3 Place a generous piece of pulp in the shell. Lay more pieces on top of the first to build up thickness. **Note:** As the layering progresses, pulp will go over the top edges of the mold's depression, spilling over on the flat areas adjacent. This can provide a nice finished edge for the shell casting.

4 When the desired thickness has been obtained, proceed with water removal, pressing, and drying (see page 11).

5 Lift the shell casting carefully. It should separate easily from the mold.

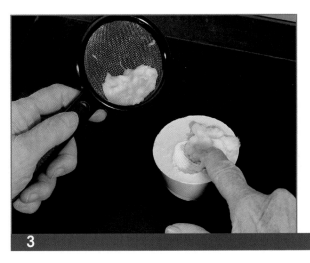

3

Metal pieces as models make quality finished molds. Metal wall plaques in relief, especially brass, are easy to find and inexpensive. They have good release properties and satisfying dimension. This project features two metal plaques; one is a 6-inch round metal plate, and the other is a rectangular brass plaque, 4-1/2 by 14-1/2 inches. The directions here are for the plate, followed by modifications for the rectangular plaque.

You Will Need

Round metal plate
Release agent
Block of modeling clay (lightly colored clays will be less likely to leach color to adjacent items)
Long flat knife
Mold medium
Water
Measuring cup
Plastic container for mixing and pouring
Paper toweling
Plastic mixing spoon
Rubber gloves

1 Spray the metal plate with a release agent. Lightly wipe off any excess.

2 Using the long flat knife, cut or work the clay into 1/2-inch thick by 1-inch wide strips.

3 Put the strips around the outside edges of the metal plate, around the detail desired for the finished casting, as shown. Join the strips' edges to prevent leakage. Framed with the clay, the metal plate is ready for the mold medium.

4 Measure 1 cup of water into the container. Put on the rubber gloves. Slowly sprinkle or sift 2 cups and 2 tablespoons of medium over the water. **Note:** This ratio of medium to water was chosen to fit the medium product being used. The example is to help give you a starting point for amounts used.

5 Let the mixture stand so the water absorbs the medium. Carefully stir with a plastic spoon. Add water or plaster in very small amounts as needed, until the mixture takes on a milkshake or mayonnaise appearance. Stir as little as needed (too much stirring hurries the setting time for the mold and creates bubbles).

6 Pour the mixture inside of the clay ring on the metal plate. Thump the metal plate to remove bubbles.

7 Let the new mold harden for at least 1 hour. Wash all utensils immediately with a hose or in a pail of water. Empty the water outdoors.

3

6

8 Remove the clay strips around the hardened mold on the metal plate. Separate the metal plate from the new mold. Put the mold aside and let it cure for at least a day.

9 After a day, wash the new mold with clear water. When dry, spray it with a release agent; wipe off excess. It is ready for a paper casting to be made on it.

The original model, the resulting mold, and the finished paper casting.

Project ... A Round Paper Cast

Choose a deckle to match the size of your round mold. Round pulp sheets are the best way to apply pulp to the new mold. Sheets can be made with a round deckle (see page 24). For the deckle, find a plastic container (anything round, like a pail or ice cream container) 6 inches in diameter or larger. The sheet method described here is recommended, but pieces, strips, or other pulp application methods described in Chapter 4 can be used for this project.

Continued on the next page.

Here is a variety of items that can be used to make round sheets. An angel food cake tin, which has a metal rim on the bottom, makes an excellent round deckle. The rim, or lip, will hold a cut-to-fit screen support of egg crate or hardware cloth.

You Will Need

Plastic tub
Egg crate or hardware cloth
Papermaking or plastic window screen
Scissors
6-inch or larger diameter round container
Sponge, terrycloth towel, and/or paper towel
Cotton linters pulp
Blender

1 Put the piece of egg crate or hardware cloth on the bottom of the tub for support and as a drain rack. Put a piece of paper-making screen or plastic window screen on top of the drain rack. Add 3 inches of water.

2 Make a round deckle by cutting the bottom off of the round container, making it open-ended.

3 Place the container top (smooth edge) down on the screen in the water.

4 Pour prepared cotton linters pulp (see page 15) into the deckle. Agitate the linters with your fingers to evenly distribute the fibers.

5 Get fingers of both hands under the support and drain rack in the water and lift. Water will drain, leaving a round pulp layer/sheet on the screen.

6 Lift off the round container. Lay the screen and pulp sheet on a surface.

7 Position the image side of the round mold down on the wet round sheet. Press the mold firmly down, squeezing out lots of water.

8 Turn the mold and pulp sheet over. Remove the screen. Proceed with water removal, pressing, and drying as described on page 11.

9 The cast can be air dried. The drying process can be shortened by placing the mold with the casting still on it in the oven with a heat setting of no more than 200 degrees. Check often. Uneven drying and the added heat may cause the casting to warp or "cockle." Never put a plaster mold in a microwave oven; a mold has to be properly formed and fired in a kiln to withstand microwaves.

3

4

6

7

A Rectangular Brass Plaque Mold...

You Will Need

Brass plaque
Release agent
Block of modeling clay
Long flat knife
Mold medium
Water
Measuring cups
Plastic container for mixing and pouring
Plastic mixing spoon
Rubber gloves
Board or layer of corrugated paperboard

The rectangular plaque needs a greater volume of mixed mold medium; the clay frame (Steps 2 and 3 on page 72) must be made strong enough to hold the greater wet mass. The directions are the as same for the round plate except:

1 Place the plaque on a board or a layer of corrugated paperboard that is cut at least 1 inch larger on all sides than the plaque.

2 Form the clay around the plaque, bonding it well to the board.

3 Pour 1-3/4 cups of water into a plastic bowl. Sprinkle or sift in 3-3/4 cups of mold medium and proceed with the mixing as previously explained. Again, adjust the mixture for water or medium.

4 Pour the medium, starting at one end of the brass plaque. Move the medium flow over the plaque, covering it evenly. Thump to remove bubbles. If the poured mass cannot be lifted to thump, remove bubbles by striking the area beside the poured mold with your fist. Let the mold harden for at least 1 hour before removing the clay frame and brass plaque from the new mold. Do not use for at least 24 hours. Then rinse the mold with clear water, dry, and spray with a release agent. It is ready for the first cast to be made on it.

5 While a disappointment, a bubble or two on the new mold is almost a given. The bubble hole can be filled with a paste of casting medium and water, which is applied with a flat toothpick.

From start to finish, mold making and paper casting involve imagination and ingenuity, but the results can be spectacular. The painted casting at far right was sprayed with flat black paint. When dry, it was sprayed with several different colors of Pearl Ex pigments that had been mixed with a matte medium, then diluted with water. The colors were sprayed on the black casting with a mouth atomizer.

...A Rectangular Paper Casting

To apply linters or other pulps to a rectangular mold, one of the pulp application methods in Chapter 4 may be used. A "made to fit" deckle is shown here. It allows you to form a thick sheet or layer that can be applied in a single application (see page 24). This allows quick and uniform application.

You Will Need

Tub with water
Mold
Release agent
Linters or pulp
Water
Blender
"Made to fit" deckle (see page 78)
Pail

1 Build the deckle (see Step 1, page 78). Build the frame to fit the outside dimensions of the brass plaque mold. Do not make a plywood bottom. Cut a screen and a support piece to fit the outside dimensions of the frame.

2 Place the wooden deckle on the screen and support piece in a tub containing at least 3 inches of water.

3 When preparing linters, increase the amount. For premeasured linters, cover the surface one and one-half times with the squares. Blend in batches of thirty with plenty of water. Pour each batch into the pail.

4 Follow Steps 4 to 9 on page 74. During the final drying step, it may be necessary to place weights on the casting (see Step 6, page 81).

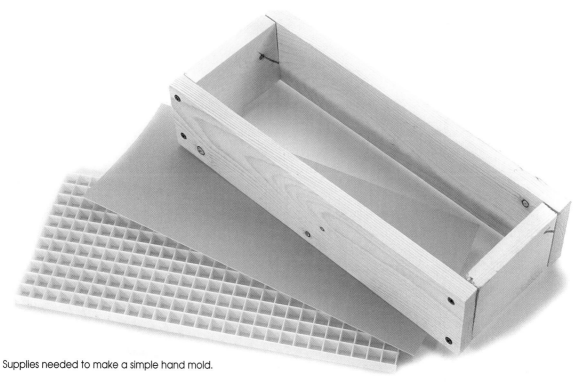

Supplies needed to make a simple hand mold.

Rules of Thumb

The tips and calculation guidelines below can be helpful when you want to make your own molds for paper casting using interesting models that come your way.

Tips for Mixing Mold Medium

- Prepare mold medium with a two-to-one ratio of plaster to water. Use the calculations below to determine how much mold medium to make.
- Always add plaster to water. Slowly **sprinkle** plaster into water; do not dump or pour.
- Stir the wet mix **as little as possible**, because stirring cause bubbles.
- Too much water in the wet mix will weaken the mold, while too much plaster creates bubbles and may cause the wet mix to set up too rapidly.
- The texture of the wet mix should resemble a thick milkshake or mayonnaise. If needed, additional plaster or water can be added before pouring the wet mix.

How to Calculate the Amount of Mold Medium to Make

Small and medium molds should be made about 1/2-inch thick and require 1 tablespoon of mold medium per square inch. Large molds should be made about 1-inch thick and require 2 tablespoons of mold medium per square inch.

1. Determine the square inches of the mold you plan to make. Multiply the length times the width of the model you are covering. The answer tells you how many tablespoons of mold medium you need for small and medium molds. Double this number for large molds.

2. It's easiest to make mold medium by the cup. There are 16 tablespoons in a cup. Divide your answer in Step 1 by 16 to determine how many cups of mold medium to make.

3. To figure out the two-to-one ratio of plaster to water you'll need for your mold, multiply your answer in Step 2 by .66. This gives you the number of cups of plaster to use to make the wet mix.

4. Subtract your answer in Step 3 from your answer in Step 2. This is the number of cups of water to use.

It's not as complicated as it sounds! Here's an applied example we used to make the wet mix for the wood carving mold featured on the following page.

1. The carving is large, 9 by 18 inches. 9 x 18 x 2 gives the number of tablespoons of wet mix needed for the carving: 324 tablespoons.

2. 324 ÷ 16 = 20, so 20 cups of wet mix are needed for this project.

3. 20 x .66 = 13, so 13 cups of plaster are needed to make the wet mix.

4. 20 - 13 = 7. The plaster will be carefully mixed into 7 cups of water. Refer to the tips above for mixing plaster into water.

A Large Mold from a Wood Carving...

The model for this large mold is a 9- by 18-inch woodcarving from Africa; it is perhaps best described as a "small" large piece. But it is interesting for its relief and variety of lines, and presents all the challenges of large pieces. The directions that follow can be used when making very large molds.

You Will Need

Wood mold
6 foot by 4-inch by 1-inch board
Drill and bit
Drywall screws
Hardboard or 1/4-inch plywood
Sheet of heavy plastic
Sealant
Release agent
Plastic window screen or hardware cloth
Bucket
Mold medium
Stick or plastic spoon
Water
Measuring cup
Sharp knife

1 Construct a box. Cut the 6-foot board into two 20-inch pieces and two 9-inch pieces. Form the pieces into a 9- by 18-inch frame. **Note:** These sizes may differ per the size of your project. Predrill holes in the 20-inch pieces on each end to accommodate the length of the project plus on-half the thickness of the board. Square the short pieces between the predrilled holes in the 20-inch pieces and secure them with drywall screws, forming a frame. Lightly tack a fitted piece of 1/4-inch hardboard or plywood to one side of the frame, making it a box (later this piece is removed, turning the box back into a frame which can be used for a deckle to make a casting with the single sheet method as described on page 76). Line the box with a sheet of heavy plastic; this will help contain the plaster if there is any leakage.

2 Seal the woodcarving. Choose a sealant that's appropriate for the model. In this case, paste wax is used to seal the wood. **Note:** Mold medium experts caution to put a durable finish on the wood if the piece has importance to the owner. They recommend a coat of spar varnish or orange shellac on the surface and edges, followed by a release agent.

3 Apply release agent. Use one of the release agents mentioned on page 18 on the model. (After being subjected to wet mold medium for a few hours, the wood carving will probably not look the same. Even though it is treated with a protective coat and sprayed with a release agent, the plaster will affect the wood carving's surface.)

4 Place the woodcarving in the box. Preferably, the fit should be quite snug; however, any casting medium oozing between the woodcarving and the plastic in the box can be trimmed later.

5 Cut the plastic window screen or hardware cloth to the size of the wood carving. Lay it aside for use in Step 7.

1

6 Measure 6-1/2 cups water into a clean pail. Sprinkle or sift 14 cups of mold medium into the water (see page 77 for notes on mixing plaster). Pour mix over prepared woodcarving, starting at one end and proceeding to the other end.

7 Thump on the table or box to remove bubbles. If a piece of cloth or plastic window screen has been prepared to give strength to the mold, it should be laid on the wet plaster immediately. It may sink into the wet mix; that's okay.

8 Do not disturb the hardening mold for at least 2 hours. Remove the screws at the ends of the box. The bottom piece is still at-tached to the wood, so the boards can only be slightly tilted for removal of the plastic-wrapped mold. Flip the whole mass over and place on your worktable. Remove the plastic, then the woodcarving. If desired, with a sharp knife, pare off any irregular edges from leakage. Let the mold cure for two days.

9 Rinse the mold off with clear water. When the mold is dry, varnish or polyurethane can be applied for preservation. Spray it with the chosen release agent and it is ready for making a paper casting.

7

Mold Medium Tips

- Bubbles in the medium are caused by too much stirring and too much water in the mixture.
- The medium becomes warm as it starts to harden, then it cools.
- The hardening or setting time of the medium is affected by the amount of water used, the depth of the mold, and the quantity of the mixture needed. The larger the project, the longer the setting time. Two hours from pouring time to releasing the mold from the model should be adequate for most projects.

8

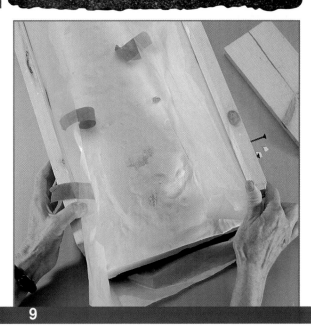

9

Project ... *A Large Paper Casting*

For very large plaster molds, the pour-the-pulp-on-the mold method might be the easiest.

You Will Need

Plastic window screen
Box (see page 78)
Plastic sheet
Pulp
Blender
Bucket
Large sponge
Terrycloth towels
Screwdriver
Blotter sheets and weights
Large mold

1 Prepare a piece of plastic window screen to fit the new mold.

2 The box that was constructed to make the plaster mold should be re-assembled. Line it with a plastic sheet. The plastic sheet should be secured to the sides of the box, which will make a type of tub to contain the water. Place the mold inside the frame.

3 Pour prepared pulp over the mold (see page 76, Step 3). Agitate fibers, being especially sure there is even distribution of fibers to the corners of the mold. Slap the surface of the slurry to bring the water to the top and help the fibers to start drifting against the mold. Lay the screen on top of the slurry of wet pulp. Place a large sponge on the puddle that starts to form on the top of the screen.

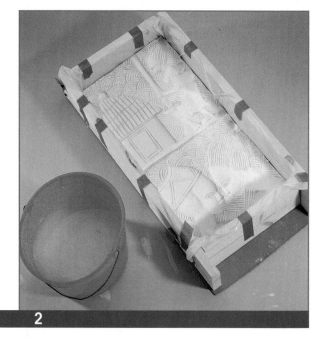

2

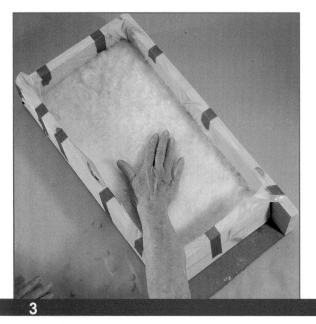

3

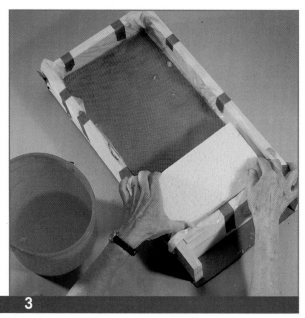

3

Wring out the sponge and continue removing water in this fashion until very little remains.

4 Peel off the screen. Continue using the sponge if water is still being removed this way. Proceed to place terrycloth towels on the cast, pressing against the towel with the flat of the hand, also pushing the pulp into the detail of the mold with the fingertips. Replace the wet towels with dry ones as long as this is effective.

5 Again remove the screws from the box. Press the boards slightly away from the mold. At this point, the decision can be made whether to try to save the box or manhandle it to remove the mold. The casting on the mold can be dried in the box, but because of the plastic and the wood being around the mold and cast, the drying time will be slowed.

6 Keep the cast weighted, either with towels or with couch (blotter) sheets with weights on them, evenly distributed over the surface. The greatest danger from having the surface curl, or cockle, is when the cast is nearly dry; it cockles because it is drying unevenly.

7 Carefully remove the cast from the mold, or it may release by itself. The cast is ready for painting, spraying, or framing as is.

A large paper casting of cotton linters is a great challenge. Hopefully the finished piece of art will be well worth the effort!

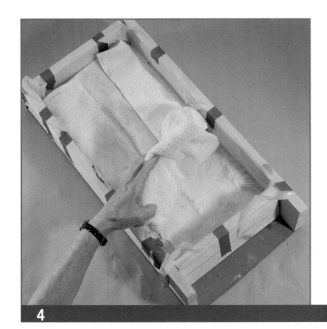

4

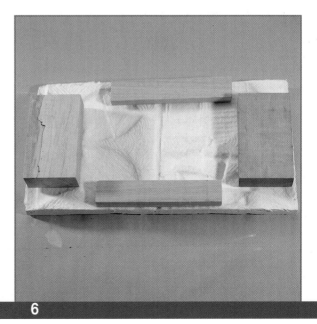

6

❋ Making Molds With Other Materials

Certain products are designed to make a cast from small commercially made molds, especially for making pins and jewelry. These products, usually clays of some type or clay combined with paper fiber, can get very hard when air dried or baked in the oven. It would seem that the hardened product would make a good mold for paper casting just as the hardened mold making medium does.

The air-dried modeling compounds do not work well for making a mold for paper casting. Re-wetting the surface of the hardened compounds causes them to become sticky or to crumble. It might be possible to paint the mold before making the paper casting, but then some of the detail is compromised.

Polymer clays harden when baked according to package directions. This product works quite well when using a model of small, simple design with broad lines and flat spaces. Models with lots of detail in the design will not work as well.

Knowing how to use polymer clays safely is important. A 12-inch piece of 1-1/4-inch PVC pipe makes a good tool to roll the clay flat. Do not use any household utensil that is used in food preparation, especially those made of wood. The toaster oven that is used to bake the molds should not be used in food preparation. Contact the manufacturer of the product for proper directions if the only oven available is your regular oven.

Project — Making a Mold from Polymer Clay

For this project, you can use buttons, rubber stamps, or anything else that you desire to make a mold.

You Will Need

Polymer clay
Model (button, rubber stamp, etc.)
PVC pipe
Toaster oven
Cotton linters or pulp
Blender
Strainer

1 Measure a piece of clay to cover the chosen model. Warm the clay in the palms of your hands to help it become pliable.

2 Roll the piece flat with the PVC pipe. Stop when the thickness is about 1/4 inch.

3 Press the rubber stamp, button, or other model evenly into the flattened compound. Observe the model from every side to make sure the impression is equally deep on all sides.

4 Carefully withdraw the model, keeping the design intact. Bake the new mold in the toaster oven, following package directions for temperature and time.

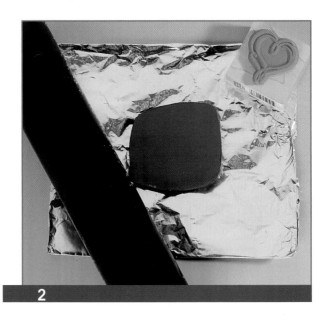

2

5 Pre-measure cotton linters or pulp to fit the size of the mold (see page 15). Blend. Pour linters into the strainer. Place pulp on the mold. Allow to dry.

6 When dry, the casting will easily separate from the polymer clay mold.

(see page 15)

Project Making a Napkin Ring Using the Cast from Polymer Clay

You Will Need

Paper casts, embellished in any desired manner
Glue gun or other adhesive
1-1/2-inch wide wire-edged ribbon, gold
Spray paint, gold
Napkins

1 Trim castings to 2-inch squares.

2 Spray the gold spray paint on both sides of each cast. Allow to dry.

3 Measure the distance around a folded napkin. Add 1/2 inch to this measurement.

4 Cut one gold ribbon to the measurement from Step 3 for each napkin. Overlap the cut edges to make a ring. Run a line of hot glue or other adhesive on each edge.

5 Attach each gold casting to a ribbon, over the glued edges, using additional hot glue or other adhesive.

The card, butterfly casts, and lampshade are made of recycled fibers, which were white envelopes and bits of pink papers blended to match the ribbon and spray paint used on the box. One cast was sprayed with gold paint. The card is cut from a sheet made on Greg Markim's 501 Papermill Pro. The heart was cut by the designer. The shade was also made on the Papermill Pro, using the scalloped lampshade template #555. PSX rubber stamps were used for the box, papers, and polymer clay mold. See Resources, on page 95, for additional product information.

See Resources, on page 95

This elegant table setting, designed by Heather Parnau, is enhanced with casts made from a rubber stamp model and ceramic molds.

Chapter Nine

Inspiration

This chapter is intended to be a smorgasbord of ideas and inspiration from young artists to some of the top paper artists in the United States. Enjoy looking at the works of art and learn from the artists' successes.

Cast paper enhanced with glitter spray.

Chapter

9

Jarrod Kastoff

Jarrod Kastoff is currently studying costume design at Columbia College of Chicago. He made this piece as a student at Wauwatosa West High School in Wauwatosa, Wisconsin.

"During an artistic lull in my high school senior year, I experimented with a papermaking set-up that I had always wanted to try. I made sheets of paper using a blender and pour hand mold, and then tore the paper into strips. I experimented with different textures I could get in the paper, and that was fun, but I wasn't sure what to do with the strips.

"My advisor, Kim Haller, suggested a fashion project since she knew I was interested in fashion design. Paper into fashion... I knew I couldn't sew on it, but I could build it on a frame—a dress dummy from the theater department was an organic idea that took on its own form.

"To make the dress, I wrapped the dummy in kitchen plastic wrap and laid on the strips. First, I tried a papier mâché glue to hold the strips together, but it didn't seem to work very well, so I used gloss medium. I knew I'd need another layer for strength and started to discover how to make brighter colors, so I put another layer of more vibrant textured paper strips over the first set.

"When the dress dried, I cut it apart on the sides and laced it up with twine for a natural look. I hung it on a walking stick with a twine hanger. The paper dress ended up becoming part of a series of dresses done in various fabrics and won a Best of Fibers Award at a University of Wisconsin High School Art Show."

Barbara Fletcher

Barbara Fletcher is a paper artist from Boston, Massachusetts. You can view her work and learn more about her at www.paperdimensions.com.

"I began my exploration of paper casting at Haystack Mountain School of Craft in Maine, where I first learned papermaking in the '80s. I was thrilled with the discovery of the casting process because I needed a method of making multiple pieces, and this was it. After taking fantasy illustration at the Rhode Island School of Design, a theme of fantasy animals began to develop in my work.

"To make my whimsical cast paper creations, I first sculpt a form in plastoscene, then make two- or three-piece molds, depending on the size of the model and the presence of undercuts. I use Hydrocal to make the molds. After removing the clay and letting the plaster cure for at least 24 hours, I begin the process of pressing wet paper pulp into the mold, making many layers for durability.

"I like to use recycled paper and bright construction paper, as well as cotton linter and abaca fibers for the casts. I don't find it necessary to use a release agent; the paper pops right out of the mold when it is dry. A scientist friend developed a tin box oven with insulation and light bulbs inside for me to dry the casts. After the work is dry, I enjoy experimenting with surface design on pieces using acrylic paints and fabric dyes with various resist techniques. Recently I have begun experimenting with illuminating paper to show off the beautiful texture."

Barbara Fletcher with suspended tropical fish and punk fish mask. Cast pieces painted with acrylics and dyes.

Photo by Jan Bindas.

Fish Fin Mask, 12 by 13 by 8 inches. Cast paper air-brushed with fabric dyes.

Photo by Gordon Bernstein.

Ornaments (left to right): Bear, Heart and Fish, Face in Leaves, Fish Face, and Heart in Hand. Color paper pulp.

David Logan

David Logan is the author of the book **Mat, Mount and Frame It Yourself.** *He also operates an e-commerce website, www.Framing4Yourself.com, where crafters and artists can acquire all of the products, materials, and know-how to mat and frame at home. For more information, contact David on his website or by phone (1-800-246-4726).*

How to Mat and Frame Dimensional Paper

You Will Need

Frame
3 sheets of mat board*
1 sheet of 1/8-inch thick foam board*
1 sheet of glass or acrylic pre-sized to your
   frame size
Measuring tape or ruler
Mat cutter
Double-sided adhesive
Utility knife
Mounting tape
Mirror clips or framers points
Brown paper
Screw eyes
Framing wire

*Mat board and foam board sheets are usually 32
   by 40 inches prior to sizing

1 Arrange the paper-cast piece on a tabletop and visualize the presentation. Measure the height and width of the presentation area you are visualizing. Visualize the four mat borders that will surround the presentation area. Add the width of the surrounding mat borders to the area. The area plus the surrounding mat borders will be the frame size.

2 Using a mat board color specifier, select the colors of the mat board you will use. There will be three mats in all: the mounting board, the over-mat of the double mat, and the under-mat of the double mat.

3 Reduce the sheets of mat board and foam board to your frame size, using the mat cutter. Further reduce the mat board that will act as the under-mat of the double mat by trimming 1/4 inch from each edge.

4 Bevel-cut a window in the mat that will act as the over-mat of the double mat. Determine the window size by subtracting the width of two mat borders from each dimension of your frame size, less an additional 1/2 inch from each dimension. After cutting, replace the drop-out piece in the window of the mat. With the mat lying face down, apply double-sided adhesive tape to the back. Avoid applying adhesive tape over the cuts.

5 Center the mat that will act as your under-mat on the back of the over-mat. Press it down on the tape.

6 Bevel-cut a window in the under-mat (now taped to the back of the over-mat).

Determine the window size by subtracting the width of two mat borders from each dimension of the frame size. When you are finished, you will have a double mat.

7 Place the mat that will act as your mounting board face down. Arrange the paper cast on the back of the mat as it will appear when viewed from the front. Mark an area for cutting a 2-inch slot in the mounting board so it will be concealed behind the paper cast in the final presentation. The slot must be about 2 inches down from where the top edge of the paper cast will be.

8 Using a utility knife and straight-edge, cut slot(s) in the mounting board. Feed 6-inch strips of mounting tape through the slot(s). Affix 2 inches of the tape against the back of the mounting board in the area above the slot(s). Let the remaining tape hang down the face of the mounting board, adhesive side out.

9 Place the double mat over the mounting board to assist in positioning the paper cast. Place the paper cast on the tape within the window of the mat. The paper cast is now mounted.

10 Cut eight strips of foam board; each strip should be 1-inch wide and roughly the length of the presentation area.

Use double-sided adhesive tape to stack and stick the strips together, forming four stacks of 1/4-inch thick strips. Apply double-sided adhesive tape to each stack and affix the stacks on the face of the mounting board, along the edges.

11 Place the double mat on top of the strips. The strips will elevate the mat off the surface of the mounting board, creating a shadowbox effect, and will work to keep the glass out of contact with the raised surface of the paper cast.

12 Place the mat/mounting board combination on the foam board backing. Place the glass (or acrylic) over the mat/mounting board/backing board combination. Place the frame over the glass/mat/mounting board/backing board combination. Turn the entire stack over and affix the components in the frame with mirror clips or framers points.

13 Attach a brown paper dust cover to the back of the frame.

14 Attach screw eyes to the back of the frame, and tie on picture framing wire. Your matted, mounted, and framed paper cast is ready to be hung!

Three rectangular paper castings made with molds created from brass plaques found in an antique store. The white cotton linter castings were matted by David Logan.

Bradley J. Parrish

Bradley J. Parrish is an internationally renowned artist with many sold-out limited editions. His works are included in such prestigious collections as the Vatican Museum in Rome and the Statue of Liberty Monument permanent collection in New York. View his work and learn more about him at www.parrishfineart.com and www.mouseking.com.

"I was painting and drawing as far back as I can remember. I work in pastel, oil, acrylic, and pen and ink. I also love to sculpt and have done some bronze work.

"One of my pastel paintings, *The Sentinel*, was chosen for a PBS auction. I got tired of seeing artists doing pencil sketches at the bottom of their prints, and I've always believed in challenging myself and the public with something unique, so I decided to make a cast paper wolf paw print to go with the limited edition print instead.

"I was given a gift by Jim Reider, founder of the Timberwolf Preservation Society, an actual paw print in plaster of Paris. I used this negative mold for the paper cast in which the final positive paper casting was made. I used pure white cotton linter for the cast to look like the paw print was in snow. The title of this paper casting is *Snow Spirit*. As a result, it was a beautiful and unique piece that accompanied the pastel painting."

The Sentinel.

Snow Spirit paper cast.

Joan Merrell

Joan Merrell is a calligrapher currently living in Jefferson City, Missouri. She has taught calligraphy for 12 years, exhibits in local and regional exhibits, and sells her work in galleries in Missouri and Utah. She is on the board of directors of the Association for the Calligraphic Arts and was chosen to be on the faculty of 2001: A Calligraphic Odyssey at the 21st International Conference of Calligraphy and Lettering Arts, where she taught calligraphic paper casting to students from as far away as Japan.

"As a professional calligrapher and busy mom who likes to find very simple ways to make elegant things, I was very interested in dry embossing, trying to get letters made only of the paper itself ever higher and more defined. When paper casting became popular in the craft world, I tried it for a graphic design class project and decided there must be a way to use the technique with calligraphy.

"I developed this method of using polymer clay rolled very thin. I use acetone to transfer a photocopy of my lettering (automatically reversing it) and then cut out the letters. I use several layers if I want different depths and then add a backing layer. This method can also be used to make three-dimensional molds on an armature, or anything that can go in the oven and take the pressure of pressing the pulp.

"I use cotton linter mostly, with bits of high-quality colored papers when I want a subtle coloration in the letters. Lots of pressing with terry towels is important to get very sharp edges and details. The polymer clay makes crisp molds, keeps precise shapes when baked, is easily cleaned or fixed with an X-acto knife after baking, and the paper pops out easily. In my opinion, Sculpey Premo is the best kind of polymer clay for this method."

Paper-cast bowl, Isaiah 11:9.

Angels, Hebrews 13:2.

Dimensional paper-cast candle with poem by Wadsworth.

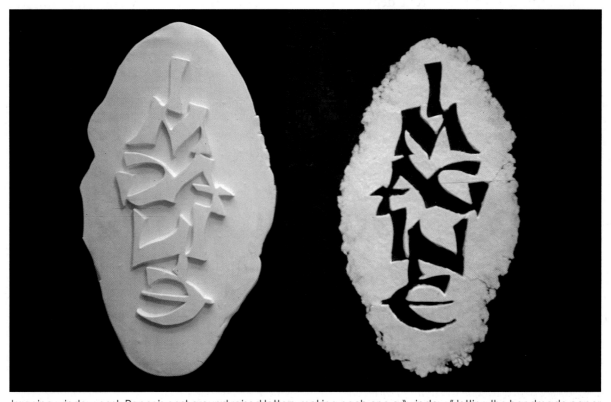

Imagine window cast. Paper is cast around raised letters, making each one a "window," letting the handmade paper background show through each one.

About the Authors

Arnold and Mabel Grummer have been "on the road" in the United States and Canada, educating and exciting anyone who would listen about paper, hand papermaking, and recycling since 1976. The itinerary has been diverse, including museums, like the Smithsonian in Washington, D.C.; the FBI Academy at Quantico, VA; and the Internal Revenue Service in Chicago. The Grummers have also made twenty consecutive years of appearances at the annual Great Lakes Logging Congress.

Arnold and Mabel have had the honor of papermaking with celebrities like Richard M. Nixon and children's author Munro Leaf and have made repeated appearances on cable television craft programs. Besides creating three papermaking videos, Arnold has written three other books related to paper.

On November 6, 1999, Arnold received a Lifetime Achievement Award for "advancing the art of papermaking and sharing your infectious joy of the craft with us all" from the prestigious paper group Friends of Dard Hunter. It is the first such award presented by the group.

Glossary

Cast (noun): An impression or shape formed in a mold or matrix.
Cast (verb): To give shape to a substance by pouring or pressing it into a mold or onto/around a matrix.
Casting (noun): See "cast."
Deckle: A frame of any form placed on top of a screen for papermaking.
Linters: The short fibers that remain on the cotton seed after ginning.
Matrix: A form from which something else (for the purpose of this book, paper casting) originates.
Model: A dimensional image rendered in metal, stone, plaster, or wood that can be "copied" in mold making.
Modeling clay: Clay of smooth consistency and of many colors which is non-toxic and does not harden.
Mold: A shaped cavity that will shape a substance pressed or poured into it.
Mold medium: Any plaster-like material for mold making that has added hardeners for strength and for picking up details.
Polymer clay: A modeling compound that bakes permanently hard in an oven.
Release agent: A substance applied to a mold or matrix surface to aid the release of a casting when dry.

Resources

Paper Making/Pulp Suppliers

Carriage House Paper
79 Guernsey St.
Brooklyn, NY 11222
718 599-7857 (and fax)
www.chpaper@aol.com

Gold's Artworks, Inc.
2100 N. Pine St.
Lumberton, NC 28358
919-739-9605

Greg Markim, Inc.
P.O. Box 13245
Milwaukee, WI 53213
414-453-1480
www.arnoldgrummer.com

Lee S. McDonald, Inc.
P.O. Box 264
Chartlestown, MA 02129
617-242-2505
617-242-8825 (fax)

Twinrocker Handmade Paper
P.O. Box 413
Brookston, IN 47923
765-563-3119
www.twinrocker.com

Mold Making Medium Suppliers

Nasco Arts & Crafts
901 Janesville Ave.
Fort Atkinson, WI 53538
www.nascofa.com

Sax Arts & Crafts
P.O. Box 510710
New Berlin, WI 53151
www.junebox.com

Casting Mold Suppliers

Cotton Press
1449 N. Angel Street, Suite 1
Layton, UT 84041
www.cottonpress.com

Greg Markim, Inc.
P.O. Box 13245
Milwaukee, WI 53213
www.arnoldgrummer.com

Hill Design (dist. by Cookie Art Exchange)
P.O. Box 4267
Manchester, NH 03108
www.cookieartexchange.com

Rycraft
4205 SW 53rd St.
Corvallis, OR 97333
www.rycraft.com

Decorative Finishes

Many of the decorative art materials, sprays, and releases featured in this book are available at local art, and hobby, paint, hardware, craft, and rubber stamp shops. Specific materials used in projects featured:

Art Institute (www.artglitter.com)
• Glitter, glue with fine tip applicator

CRAF-T Products (www.craf-tproducts.com)
• Chalks, rub on metallics

PSX (www.psxdesign.com)
• Rubber stamps used in several projects

USArtquest (www.usartquest.com)
• Duo-embellishing gilding adhesive
• Gildenglitz™ gilding supplies

Index